# GETTING TO KNOW
# DOGS

Choosing, Caring For, and Living With Man's Best Friend

DIANA ANDERSEN

**Animalinfo Publications**
**February 2014**

© Animalinfo Publications 2014

Animalinfo Publications
PO Box 605,
Kalamunda,
WA 6976 Australia

ISBN 978 1 921537 24 0

All rights reserved. No part of this publication may be reproduced, stored in any retrieval system, or transmitted in any form, by any means without the permission of Animalinfo Publications

## Disclaimer

*This book is intended for information only. The publisher and author do not imply any results to those using this book, nor are they responsible for any results brought about by the usage of the information contained herein. The publisher and author disclaim any personal liability, loss, or risk incurred as a result of the use of any information or advice contained herein either directly or indirectly. Furthermore, the publisher and author do not guarantee that the holder of this information will generate the same results as each dog is an individual that may have many variables.*

**Photography - Diana Andersen, Animalinfo Publications**

**Front Cover:** Keeshonds at the Beach
**Back Cover:** German Shorthaired Pointer
**Below:** Havanese Dog

# Contents

## About the Author — 9
Diana Andersen — 9

## Acknowledgements — 11
Cathy Lambert, Rae Joy & Lisa Mantellato — 11
Cindy Ludwig, Canine Connection LLC — 11

## Introduction — 13
Cute isn't he? But is he the Right Dog for You? — 13

## Are You Ready For a Dog? — 15
History of the Domestic Dog — 15
Dog Behaviour — 16
Assessing Your Own Situation — 18
  Dogs Cost Money! — 18
  Dogs Need Exercise! — 18
  Dogs Need Training! — 19
Purebred Versus Mixed Breed — 20
One Dog or Two — 22

## Popular Dog Breeds — 25
About Dog Breeds — 25
Why are Some Breeds More Popular? — 26
How Do I Decide? — 27
  Size — 27
    Very Small Breeds (Toys) — 27
    Small to Medium Breeds — 29
    Medium to Large — 32
    Very Large Breeds — 35
  Coat — 37
  Temperament — 42
  Health — 44
Rare Breeds — 47

## Finding Your New Dog — 51
- Breeders of Purebred Dogs — 51
- Pet Shops — 53
- Rescue Shelters — 55

## Selecting a Healthy Puppy — 59
- What Should You Expect From a Supplier? — 59
- Veterinary Certification — 61
- Pedigree Papers and Contracts — 61
- Available Health Screening — 63
- Visual Examination — 64

## Bringing Your Puppy Home — 71
- Preparing For Your New Puppy — 71
- The First Days — 73
- Diets and Feeding Regime — 75
- Toilet Training — 80
- Lead Training — 83
- Keeping Your Puppy Safe — 84

## Getting an Adult Dog — 87
- Selecting an Adult Dog — 87
- Meeting Other Family Members — 89
- Establishing a Routine — 89
- Adopting an Older Dog — 91

## Feeding Your Dog — 95
- Introduction — 95
- Commercial Diets — 96
  - Protein — 96
  - Carbohydrates — 96
  - Fibre — 97
  - Fats and Oils — 97
  - Supplements — 97

| | |
|---|---|
| Fruit and Vegetables, Flavours, and Sweeteners | 97 |
| Preservatives | 98 |
| Fresh Foods | 98 |
| Special Needs | 101 |
| Older Dogs | 101 |
| Overweight Dogs | 102 |
| Food allergies and Special Diets | 104 |

# Keeping Your Dog Healthy 107

| | |
|---|---|
| Visual Examination | 107 |
| Vaccinations | 108 |
| Core | 110 |
| Non-Core | 110 |
| Canine Distemper Virus (CDV) | 111 |
| Rabies | 111 |
| Bordetella | 112 |
| Canine Parvovirus | 112 |
| Infectious Hepatitis | 112 |
| Parainfluenza and Adenovirus Type 2 | 113 |
| Lyme Disease | 113 |
| Endoparasites & Ectoparasites | 114 |
| Heartworm | 114 |
| Intestinal Worms | 115 |
| Roundworms *(Toxocara canis & Toxascaris leonina)* | 116 |
| Hookworms *(Ancylostoma caninum, Ancylostoma braziliens)* | 117 |
| Whipworms *(Trichuris vulpis)* | 119 |
| Tapeworms *(Dipylidium caninum)* | 120 |
| Hydatid Tapeworms *(Echinococcus granulosis)* | 120 |
| Fleas | 121 |
| Ticks | 123 |
| Mites | 123 |
| Demodex mites | 123 |
| Sarcoptes mites | 123 |

| | |
|---|---:|
|     Ear Mites | 123 |
| Teeth and Nails | 124 |
|   Dental Care | 124 |
|   Nail Trimming | 125 |
| Grooming | 127 |
|   Brushing and Trimming | 127 |
|   Bathing | 131 |
|   Ear Cleaning | 133 |
| Anal Glands | 134 |
| Sterilisation | 135 |
| Exercise and Play | 137 |

## Common Health Issues — 143

| | |
|---|---:|
| Introduction | 143 |
| Arthritis | 143 |
| Cancer | 145 |
| Cataracts | 149 |
| Diabetes Mellitus (Type I Diabetes) | 151 |
| Heart Disease | 152 |
| Genetic Disease – An Introduction | 153 |

## Responsible Ownership — 157

| | |
|---|---:|
| Basic Training and Obedience | 157 |
| Being a Good Neighbour | 160 |
| Respecting Wildlife and the Environment | 163 |
| Irresponsible Practices | 164 |
| Old Age | 165 |

## References & Resources — 167

| | |
|---|---:|
| General Resources | 167 |
|   National Kennel Clubs and Councils | 167 |
|   Dog Clubs and Clubs for the Mixed Breeds | 167 |
|   Training Resources | 168 |

| | |
|---|---:|
| Additional General Resources | 168 |
| Health Resources | 169 |
|     Disease Testing and Information Organisations | 169 |
|         UNITED STATES | 169 |
|             Health Registries | |
|             Testing Agencies | |
|         ENGLAND | 170 |
|             Health Registries | |
|             Testing Agencies | |
|         AUSTRALIA | 170 |
|             Health Registries | |
|             Testing Agencies | |
|     National Veterinary Associations | 171 |
|     Further Reading | 171 |
|     Pet Loss Support | 171 |
|     Cancer Information | 172 |
|     Additional Health Resources | 172 |
| Other Titles from Animalinfo Publications | 174 |

*One of my wonderful Australian Cattle Dogs, 'Tyson'.*

# About the Author

www.animalinfo.com.au

*Animalinfo Publications*

## Diana Andersen

Although I began my working life as a professional designer with a background in photography, I have always been passionate about animals and have never been without their companionship. This passion for animals eventually became a profession, working as a zoo keeper while also breeding birds at home, doing rescue and rehabilitation for endangered cockatoos, and breeding and showing Australian Cattle Dogs, purely for the enjoyment of participating in a recreational activity with my dogs.

As my expertise with animals increased so did requests for me to share the information with others through speaking engagements, magazine articles, and books. I could never say no to anyone who called for advice on problems relating to their animals. With people turning to the internet for animal information, I became concerned, and frustrated at times, with the amount of inaccurate information being circulated. Information was becoming available from people that had little real experience or expertise with the animals they were writing about. While I could distinguish a great deal of what was good from what wasn't, I doubted that many less experienced people could.

Although my books had been published by other companies in the past, I founded Animalinfo Publications in 2007. I felt that my design, photography and web skills could be used to my advantage to produce quality books, e-books and other information products that would meet and surpass international standards. The aim was to provide predominantly online information which was accurate, well researched, and sourced from professionals working with animals. I believe that fewer animals would be in need of rescue and re-homing if people made well informed decisions about the animals that they intend to share their lives with and are provided with good information on maintaining their health and wellbeing.

Producing this book and the others available from Animalinfo Publications has also allowed me to spend more time on another of my passions, observing and capturing the spirit of animals through the camera lens. I hope you enjoy the information and photographs provided in this book, and please, visit our website at www.animalinfo.com.au.

Red and White Border Collies

# Acknowledgements

*Great Dane*

### Cathy Lambert, Rae Joy & Lisa Mantellato

Cathy, Rae and Lisa have provided invaluable support in establishing Animalinfo Publications. They have all devoted their professional, and much of their personal lives, to working with animals. Cathy and Lisa work with native species breeding programs at Perth Zoo in Western Australia, breeding endangered species for release back into their native habitat, and Rae, a qualified vet nurse, worked with the Animals Asia Foundation at the Moon Bear Rescue Centre in Vietnam. Amongst other things, they have collectively provided much of the research needed for the health sections of this book and provided a great deal of the health and breed information that can be found on our website.

### Cindy Ludwig, Canine Connection LLC

Cindy Ludwig, M.A. is a Karen Pryor Academy Certified Training Partner based in Dubuque, Iowa specialising in force-free positive reinforcement training. Apart from behaviour consultation, modification and training classes, Cindy is also involved with service and therapy dog training and assessment. Her expertise and advice has been invaluable in reviewing the behaviour and training information contained in this book. Cindy also contributes articles to the Animalinfo Publications website. Cindy's contact details can be found in the 'Resources' section at the end of this book.

*Golden Retriever*

*Australian Cattle Dog 'Rusty' at 13 years of age taking his favourite toy out for a spin! This breed is tenacious, energetic and needs room to move.*

# Introduction

*Australian Cattle Dog Puppy*

## Cute isn't he? But is he the right dog for you?

So you have decided to get a puppy? If the answer is yes, then you have already made your first mistake! You should have said that you have decided to get a dog. Puppies physically mature at a truly alarming rate. Unfortunately, from a behavioural standpoint, they can take a great deal longer to reach maturity. While they are no longer small, cute and cuddly, they can still have unexpected accidents on the floor, chew up inappropriate and valuable items, and invent a multitude of other little activities designed to gain your attention and try your patience!

The biggest mistake people make is to look for a puppy before realistically assessing their own situation to determine whether they are ready to bring a dog into their family and can meet the responsibilities associated with owning a dog. Puppies are cute - there can be no argument about that. However, if you purchased the puppy pictured above because you just couldn't resist, and you live in a small inner city townhouse, you have probably just made a terrible mistake.

It's not that there is anything wrong with the breed, far from it. However, this is a working breed that needs room to move, is tenacious and energetic, and likes to be with its owner at all times. Confined to a small yard and left alone all day, this breed, and many others, will often become noisy and destructive.

Owning a dog can be a rewarding experience that I thoroughly recommend but only if you choose the right companion for your situation. They are not a status symbol, something to match the decor of your house, or a disposable item to be dropped of at the local rescue shelter when you can't afford to meet its needs, or it has become an inconvenience. To get the most out of owning a dog, first and foremost you need to be realistic!

*To get the most out of owning a dog, it is important to choose a dog whose temperament and activity level is suited to your lifestyle.*

*Papillon*
*Try to base your choice of companion on your lifestyle, not on how beautiful or cute a dog or a breed may be.*

# Are you ready for a dog?

## History of the Domestic Dog

Before deciding on whether to include a dog in your life, it is important to understand a little about the nature and history of dogs. There are a number of theories on the origin of the domestic dog. Studies have been done on the mitochondrial DNA of dogs that suggest that the domestication of dogs originated in East Asia. Recent studies involving more advanced techniques, used to scan for genetic disease in humans, have been used to analyze the DNA of wolves from around the world and many domestic dog breeds. In contrast to the earlier study, this research puts the domestication of dogs in the Middle East in the same region, and around the same time, as the domestication of plants and other animals. This is further supported by archaeological evidence with some of the oldest dog remains being found in the Middle East dating from 12,000 years ago.

A large collection of wolf and dog genomes were examined for similarities by Bridgett M. vonHoldt and Robert K. Wayne, a research team from the University of California. Samples from the Middle East showed the greatest similarities. However, there were other areas of overlap in East Asia that suggested that dogs originating from domesticated wolves in the Middle East spread to East Asia where they were then crossed back to wolves. It is believed that the association of humans and wolves

*Wire Fox Terrier*

*Mexican Wolf (Canis lupus baileyi) Photo - Jim Clark US Fish & Wildlife Service*

began with scavenging wolves following humans to feed off their food scraps, injured prey and carcasses. Smaller, less threatening animals following hunter gatherers are thought to have become dependent on humans. The benefit to humans was that the wolves probably provided a warning system against attack. It is thought that they may have been utilised as sentries when humans first began to settle around 15,000 years ago. At this time humans began to intervene in their breeding patterns, selecting for smaller size and other attributes that made them more useful and suitable for integration into human society. They may also have been domesticated to provide a food source, or to act as beasts of burden like huskies pulling sleds for the Inuit.

As these relationships developed, dogs continued to be more selectively bred to suit the needs of humans. Crossing wolves and dogs has occurred as recently as 1955 with the commencement of a breeding program aimed at producing a dog for use in the military. This breed, known as Czechoslovakian Wolfdogs, was officially recognised as a national breed in 1982 and was developed by crossing working line German Shepherds with Carpathian Wolves. However, in most situations wolf traits would have been a disadvantage in dogs, particularly in those breeds that were needed to guard and herd.

*Czechoslovakian Wolfdogs, a breed developed from crossing working line German Shepherd Dogs with Carpathian Wolves, originally for use in the military. Photo - Margo Peron*

In the Victorian era, dog fanciers began to selectively breed and show dogs, leading to the large variation of breeds that we see today. In modern breeds, where companionship is the primary function of a vast majority of dogs, there is a greater emphasis on breeding for appearance and temperament. As a result, new breeds are still emerging although some have also disappeared.

## Dog Behaviour

While domestic dogs now vary greatly in appearance, their wolf ancestry still plays a part in their behaviour. Canines, like humans, are social creatures, with a hierarchical structure to their groups. A person contemplating the purchase of a toy breed may consider the ancestry of dogs to be irrelevant, but this would be a mistake. My long association with dogs has resulted in more than one bite. However, the only bite I have ever received, that was intended to cause me harm, was from a toy breed. Regardless of size or breed, dogs are still dogs, sharing many of the same genetic traits and behavioural tendencies. The desire to belong to a social group is probably the strongest genetic trait that has been retained, and the one that makes them such good companions for humans.

While some cope well without the constant company of their owners, most dogs prefer not to be alone and many of the behavioural problems that people experience, such as barking and destructive behaviour, result from being alone with insufficient mental stimulation, inadequate training, and often having also had inadequate exercise. When you encounter undesirable behaviours in your dog, consider tracing the origins back to wild behaviour, in an effort to better understand them. For instance, when they dig up your roses to bury a bone, they are responding to a powerful innate urge to store food, as a safeguard against hunger when prey is scarce. Understanding these instincts may help you make some compromises when living together, or allow you to modify some of your dog's behaviours that you just can't live with.

*While domestic dogs now vary greatly in appearance, their wolf ancestry still plays a part in their behaviour.*

When you bring a dog into your home it needs to become part of your family. Many dogs are stronger than humans and therefore they must learn acceptable behaviour towards all family members. This doesn't mean being aggressive or intimidating. It means developing a relationship where your dog knows its boundaries. You must be clear and consistent with what you expect from your dog. Trainers using positive reinforcement methods work from the standpoint that the owner is a 'benevolent leader' responsible for teaching the dog to work for food and attention rather than receiving valuable resources on demand, not because they are 'above' the dog but because it is natural and emotionally healthy in a family structure. If you do not intend to allow your dog to become part of your family, your home, and your daily routine, consider your decision carefully. You may be making a serious mistake!

*Many dogs are stronger than humans and therefore they must learn acceptable behaviour towards all family members.*

## Assessing Your Own Situation

### Dogs Cost Money!

It's not just the purchase price you need to consider but also the cost of good food, vaccinations, wormers, fencing and housing. There are also a multitude of accessories now available, and the costs of emergency visits to the vet. If you think you need to be unlucky for your dog to require a vet visit, ask yourself how many times you have needed to go to the doctor yourself in the past ten to fifteen years. It happens. They are no different from us in that regard. Ask yourself if you could stand to see your dog suffer if it needed attention just because you couldn't afford a visit to the vet. Just for good measure, they always get sick on a weekend when it costs more to visit the vet!

### Dogs Need Exercise!

There is a little room to move here depending on the breed you choose. For instance, a toy breed may not be as keen to run a marathon as a working breed but like humans, no exercise at all is going to lead to poor health issues. Going for a walk is not only good exercise, but provides your dog with companionship, some mental stimulation and breaks the boredom of the day. Boredom leads to behavioural problems regardless of the size and activity level of the breed. You need to be sure that you have the time and inclination to spend some time out of the house with your dog. Be realistic when choosing your dog. If you have only a small backyard in a heavily populated area, don't buy a large active dog that is going to be climbing the walls with boredom and barking continuously because it is the only release it has against the frustration of its confinement.

*Lakeland Terrier*
*Dogs love and need to exercise.*

## Dogs Need Training!

What's it like owning a puppy? It's a bit like getting a very young child that can run a lot faster than you! You need to get this bundle of mischief under control as soon as possible. It doesn't need to take a lot of time if you aren't interested in competitive obedience training, but it does require some effort to make your dog aware of the boundaries and to learn acceptable behaviour. Puppies need to play and chew and this is just an unavoidable fact of life. They see no difference between their toys and your best shoes and clothes, unless someone teaches them. Rather than walking at a reasonable pace, they seem to believe that there is some sort of reward for getting to wherever they are going at ninety miles an hour, dragging their owner along behind them. Training will help

*By eight weeks of age puppies are ready for mischief.*

resolve and prevent these issues. There are many organisations that teach obedience, as well as books and videos to help you. Training should be considered a commitment for the life of your dog and factored into the costs of bringing a dog into your family. Only you can decide if you have the time and inclination and resources to fulfil this requirement of owning a dog but dogs will learn whether we teach them or not, so why not teach them desirable behaviours. Clicker training, a type of positive reinforcement training is highly recommended. You will find a number of links in the Resources section to help you get started with clicker training.

## Purebred Versus Mixed Breed

Having been a breeder of purebred dogs in the past you would expect me to automatically recommend that you purchase a purebred. The reality is that I like all dogs and I have certainly met some delightful mixed breed 'mutts' over the years. However, rescue shelters are full of less successful crosses that are often the result of uncontrolled breeding between breeds that should never have been crossed. Although all dogs are individuals, often dogs within a breed share characteristics. For instance, Jack Russell Terriers have the feisty nature of a terrier and can be quite energetic and tenacious but their small stature makes them manageable. Add size and weight by crossing them with a large breed and you may end up with a dog that is much more difficult to control.

If you decide on a purebred dog then you can at least do some research on the characteristics of that breed, visit dog shows and breeders, and get a feel for the temperament of a particular bloodline. With crossbred puppies it really is pot luck. If you see the parents you may get some idea of how big the dog may grow and what its personality might be, but if not, you will have no idea of what you might end up with. I am not the sort of person who can simply re-home a dog once it has become part of the family, so if you are anything like me then you should choose carefully.

If you want to get a mixed breed dog then I suggest visiting a rescue shelter. These non-profit organisations take in many unwanted dogs, including purebreds, each year. They are unable to re-home many of them leaving euthanasia as the only other option. On the down side, many of

*Mixed breed puppies are cute but it may be impossible to judge what their final size and appearance may be.*

these dogs have 'baggage' from previous owners who may have mistreated them, but on the up side, you can get a better idea of what you are buying in terms of looks and personality as the dogs are often older. You also miss out on the difficulties of dealing with a puppy and many behavioural issues can be corrected with patience, care and the help of trainers and training organisations.

Puppies bred from healthy mothers get a good start in life as a result of the good body condition of their mothers. Being wormed regularly, and being brought up on a good diet, will also help pups have fewer health issues as they get older. Of course, there are breeders of purebred dogs that may not care for their animals as well as they should. However, as a general rule, people who exhibit their dogs and are prepared to sell them with pedigree papers, take excellent care of their breeding stock and their puppies. Their reputation is at stake and they are often contemplating keeping a pup from the litter themselves, which may be their next champion, so they can't afford not to care for their dogs well. By buying a purebred dog from a registered breeder who breeds selectively and infrequently, you may be more likely to get a puppy that has been fed well, vaccinated, wormed at the appropriate time, and had a health check by a vet.

There has been a recent trend to produce weird and wonderful new combinations of cute mixed breeds, usually utilising the smaller, fluffy breeds. These have some truly weird and wonderful price tags as well! They are often produced in 'puppy mills' where dogs may be kept in crowded, unsanitary and unhealthy conditions. Females are bred every time they come in season and puppies are sold when they are very young into pet shops where impulse buying often lands puppies in homes where they are not suited. As far as I am concerned, these dogs are simply mixed breeds and the same warnings I have already mentioned also apply.

*There has been a recent trend to create mixed breeds utilising the smaller fluffy breeds such as this Shih Tzu/ King Charles Spaniel cross.*

Responsible purebred dog breeders recognise that many dog breeds have genetic weaknesses and disease issues that require work to eliminate them from the breed through genetic testing and selective breeding. No such care is taken in the production of these designer dogs, nor is any consideration given to how one genetic defect may affect another when the two breeds are bred together. No consideration is given to whether the coat will be manageable when two different coat types are mixed. Many genetic diseases affect more than one breed so being a mixed breed does not automatically eliminate the possibility of genetic disease. Breeds like purebred Poodles and purebred Cavalier King Charles Spaniels are probably cuter than crosses between the two, known as 'Cavoodles' anyway!

Whatever your decision might be, make sure you do your research on the dog or breed you are thinking of getting. Rescue shelters have more than enough unwanted dogs and if people took more care in their choice of dog and their responsibilities as dog owners, perhaps they would have fewer dogs to care for, re-home or otherwise dispose of.

## One Dog or Two

For a number of reasons, many people opt to share their lives with two dogs. This can be beneficial for the dog, particularly in households where there is no one at home during the day, but it should not be considered a solution to not having enough time to spend with your dog. Two dogs still need walks, play time, and other forms of human interaction. If you have insufficient time for one dog, you probably have even less for two. Two dogs however, can play vigorously together, allowing you to relax at the end of a long day at work and watch while the dogs participate in the more physical aspects of play.

*Two dogs can play vigorously together.*

Some people get a second dog when the first is getting older. Often the reason for this is to lessen the sense of loss when the older dog dies, however bringing a new puppy that gets lots of attention, into the home of an older single dog, can result in competition between the two. You need to make sure that the older dog is not forgotten and still gets plenty of attention. Another reason is that the owners hope to model the pup's behaviour on the older dog, helping it to learn acceptable behaviour. Two puppies can certainly get up to all sorts of trouble without an adult dog to socialise with. However, just remember, puppies are just as quick or quicker to learn unacceptable behaviour from an older dog. If your older dog has some bad habits then there is a good chance the pup may adopt the same habits.

For the sake of your family and your dogs, if you aim to be a two dog household consider the timing and consequences of your decision carefully before introducing a second dog.

*Shiba Inu*
*Puppies will model their behaviour on an older dog. However, they can also learn bad habits.*

*When you bring a dog into your home it needs to become part of your family.*

# Popular Dog Breeds

## About Dog Breeds

Dog breeds are categorised into ten groups by the Fédération Cynologique Internationale (FCI), an organisation with a membership of eighty four countries. By establishing common nomenclature and ensuring that the pedigrees of all participating countries are recognised, the organisation facilitates the showing and breeding of dogs worldwide amongst member countries. The breeds are often grouped according to their ancestral dog types, or by their purpose, such as 'sheepdogs'. Kennel clubs around the world also group dogs, even if they are not a member of the FCI, though most use only seven groups and these may vary in name. Dogs may also be grouped differently in different countries. For instance, the American Kennel Club has a working group and a herding group. In contrast, the Australian National Kennel Council has a working group and a utility group, but no herding group. Therefore, herding breeds such as Border Collies are judged in the herding group in the US, but judged in the working group in Australia.

Although this grouping of breeds may give some insight into the heritage and nature of the breeds grouped together, there are many variations within these groups relating to size, coat, temperament, and appearance. For instance, in the terrier group there are very large breeds such as the Airedale, but also small

*Yorkshire Terrier*

*Jack Russell Terriers*

terriers like the Jack Russell. Coats may also vary greatly within a breed group from the long silky coats of the Maltese to the very short smooth coat of the Miniature Pinscher, both members of the toy group in most countries.

Within a breed there can also be variations both in physical appearance and temperament, resulting from the bloodlines used by the breeder. Selecting a breeder carefully can help you find a dog with a good temperament that is suited to your lifestyle. Of course, how you raise and train your dog will also impact on the relationship you have with your dog, so don't be too quick to blame the breeder if you encounter problems. If you experience problems relating to health or behaviour, it is best to speak to the breeder or seek professional advice sooner rather than later.

## Why are Some Breeds More Popular?

If you search the internet for 'popular dog breeds' you will get a variety of lists relating to the number of dogs registered worldwide. However, the reasons that a breed becomes popular can be based on a number of factors.

The Labrador is popular due to its well earned reputation of being a great family dog. Its characteristic good nature, short easy care coat, and trainability are all contributing factors. With other breeds, popularity may be based on the fact that the breed has become fashionable to own. This is the very worst reason to choose a particular breed, particularly if the breed is one with a more difficult temperament, or a difficult coat to care for. For example, Afghan Hounds became very popular in the 1970s but most people do not have the time or the inclination to care for the long coat that makes the Afghan so appealing.

*Some breeds like Labradors (left) are popular because they are great family dogs. Others, like the popularity of Afghan Hounds (right) in the 1970s, become popular because they are fashionable to own, regardless of the difficulties associated with owning one.*

Breeds that become popular for the wrong reasons are far more likely to end up in rescue or need re-homing. I am not suggesting that breeds with difficult coats, tenacious temperaments or high activity levels should be avoided at all costs but before choosing a breed, popular or otherwise, you should assess whether you have the time and resources needed to properly care for the particular breed that you are interested in.

## How Do I Decide?

It is strongly recommended that you do some research on breeds that you are considering before looking at puppies or available dogs. However, with so many breeds to choose from it can be hard to know where to begin. There are four main areas that you need to consider which should help you narrow your search. These are size, coat, temperament and health.

### Size

Every breed has an ideal size range defined by the breed standard which is used for judging purposes. In breed standards, the size of the dog in most breeds is measured at the wither, the highest point of the shoulder, but for very small breeds, size may be determined by weight instead. For the purposes of this chapter I will group breeds much more loosely as very small, often referred to as toys, small to medium, medium to large, and very large for breeds referred to as giant.

### Very Small Breeds (Toys)

There are quite a few breeds that fall into the category of very small. These breeds are referred to as 'toy' breeds and are usually judged in this group but some, like Toy Poodles, are judged in the non-sporting group along with the other larger Poodle varieties. There are also some small terriers such as the Yorkshire Terrier, English Toy Terrier, and the Australian Silky Terrier that are often judged in the toy group rather than in the terrier group. Other breeds like the Shih Tzu are shown in the toy

*Yorkshire Terriers are amongst the popular toy dog breeds.*

group in the US but are judged in the non-sporting group in other countries. Shih Tzu would be at the larger end of this group with substantial body weight and structure in comparison to the small breeds like Chihuahuas and Miniature Pinschers.

As many of the traditional uses for larger dogs are no longer relevant in today's society, companionship has become the primary function of dogs. Toy breeds have become increasingly popular as companion dogs as their small size makes them very easy to accommodate in inner city situations, and they are less expensive to feed. Some of the most popular toy breeds include the Yorkshire Terrier, Maltese, Chihuahua, Pug, Cavalier King Charles Spaniel and Papillon. Toy breeds are particularly well suited to older people who do not have the physical strength to deal with a larger stronger dog.

*Long-haired Chihuahua*

There is very little about the appearance of small breeds that is reminiscent of their wolf ancestry. Many of the breeds are the product of more intensive selective breeding than other, larger breeds and can therefore potentially have genetic health issues that need careful selection to avoid when purchasing a puppy. Some have very long coats that will require regular grooming and clipping to maintain. Others, like Miniature Pinschers and Italian Greyhounds have very fine coats and are inclined to feel the cold. In general, very small breeds need to share your home. If you want a dog that is housed outside all the time, don't choose a toy breed. That doesn't mean that they never see the outside world. Toy dogs are still dogs and enjoy a walk and can be trained.

Keeping small breeds confined to a yard can be difficult. They have a knack of squeezing through very small gaps and they are not known for their road sense. They also have the reputation of being noisy, excitable, aggressive, and in many cases nervous. Studies have shown that this is more likely to be associated with the actions of the owner, than with the breed or size of the dog. Inconsistency in interactions, and more frequent use of punishment has been shown to be associated with increased incidence of aggression and excitability. Inadequate play and training have also been shown to be contributing factors and the study concluded that small dog owners could significantly improve their dog's obedience if they engaged in more frequent play and training sessions, and improved the consistency of their interactions.

*Pugs (top), Papillon (bottom left) and Maltese (bottom right) are popular toy breeds.*

## Small to Medium Breeds

It is difficult to categorise dogs as small or medium as there are breeds of all shapes and sizes that increase gradually in either height, or weight, or both. For this group I am referring to dogs that are often just outside the toy group such as Miniature Poodles, Miniature Schnauzers, Miniature Dachshunds, heavier short breeds like Welsh Corgis, many terriers, and small working breeds like Shetland Sheepdogs.

There are many beautiful dogs amongst the small to medium breeds, both in appearance and temperament. Several small to medium breeds have featured prominently in the

Popular Dog Breeds 29

popularity lists over the past few years though this varies between countries. These include Beagles, English Bulldogs, Miniature Poodles, Shetland Sheepdogs and Cocker Spaniels, both English and American. There are also quite a few others to choose from. A number of popular terriers such as Staffordshire Bull Terriers, Smooth Fox Terriers, and West Highland White Terriers fall into this size group as well.

*Shetland Sheepdogs, a beautiful small breed.*

Many of the breeds have been developed as companion dogs, rather than working dogs. However, some still have a working heritage in herding, hunting or retrieving, and the Staffordshire Bull Terrier and the Bulldog have less appealing histories in blood sports such as dog fighting, and bull and bear baiting in the case of the Bulldog.

Like the smaller breeds in the toy group, the smaller size of these breeds may make them easier to accommodate in high density modern living conditions. They still need room to move and should be exercised on a regular basis. Like larger working breeds, those medium sized breeds with a working heritage can easily get bored. Some research into the history of the breed is also highly recommended. For instance, Beagles are generally very sound little dogs with good temperaments but they were originally developed as a pack hunting dog. As a result they are often unhappy and potentially noisy if left alone for long periods, so a Beagle may not be the best choice if you only want a single dog.

Like toy breeds, many are the product of more intensive selective breeding and therefore can also have potential genetic health issues. Finding a good breeder that spends the time and money on genetic health testing is well worth the effort. French Bulldogs and English

Bulldogs are also brachycephalic (short nosed) breeds and you should be aware of the difficulties associated with this condition before deciding to get one.

*Popular small to medium breeds include English Bulldogs (top left), Beagles (top right) and Staffordshire Bull Terriers (below).*

## Medium to Large

This group includes medium height working breeds like Border Collies, Australian Kelpies and Australian Cattle Dogs, many Gundogs like Labradors, taller, more muscular and elegant breeds like Dobermanns, through to breeds that are very large but not considered 'giant'. Many medium to large dogs come from breeds that were developed to work, hunt and retrieve. Many of these breeds make wonderful family pets and often feature high in the popular breed lists like Labrador Retrievers, Boxers and Golden Retrievers. Because of their working heritage though, some may still have a high working drive and be very active.

As dogs are more in demand as family companions these days, many breeders will breed selectively for dogs with relaxed and friendly temperaments. However, all these breeds will need regular exercise to burn off energy and keep them fit and healthy. There are some breeders who still breed from working lines, particularly in breeds that are still used to guard and herd, so it is best to choose carefully if you aren't interested in the sports and activities that they were bred for. Discuss the temperament and activity levels of the breeder's lines when making enquiries about the dogs they have available. There are breeders who will refuse working line puppies to pet homes. This decision should be respected as it is in the best interest of the dog and the new owner.

*Golden Retriever competing in retrieving trials.*
*Dogs bred from working lines can still excel in the work they originally bred for.*

While medium to large breeds are more easily accommodated than giant breeds, they can still wreak havoc in a small house or yard if not properly trained. Boredom can be an issue as well if they are left confined with inadequate exercise. On the other hand many adapt extremely well to training, particularly if the breed was developed to work. The Border

Collie breed is considered the smartest of all the breeds, followed closely behind by other large breeds that were all developed to assist humans, such as Dobermanns and German Shepherds. Standard Poodles, generally ranked as the second smartest breed, were also originally bred to retrieve but have been selectively bred as companion dogs for many generations.

Many medium to large breeds are physically very strong so the importance of training cannot be overstated, particularly if you want to let your dog off lead in public. To avoid being considered a threat to humans and other dogs they must remain under control. At home, you must also ensure that you have adequate fencing to contain your dogs as well.

*The Border Collie is considered the smartest of all the breeds.*

*Labrador Retrievers are amongst the most popular dog breeds and make wonderful family pets like many other medium to large breeds.*

Even if your dog is not aggressive to other dogs, many large breeds will defend themselves when attacked by another dog, a situation which is extremely difficult and dangerous to diffuse. Breed specific legislation is becoming a reality for many large breeds around the world, largely due to the activities of irresponsible owners who are unable to control their dogs.

*Rottweiler*
*Training is essential to keep large breeds under control.*

*Boxers are a medium to large breed that is popular in many countries.*

There are a number of beautiful Sighthounds amongst the medium to large breeds such as Greyhounds, Salukis, Afghans, Borzois and Pharaoh Hounds. These elegant hounds often have very mellow temperaments and are relaxed and easy to live with. They are generally okay with other dogs provided they have been socialised from an early age, but due to their hunting heritage, they may not be the best choice around other small pets. They should be kept leashed in public areas due to their inclination to chase things that

*Whippet*
*Sighthounds need to be kept on a leash.*

move and your home should be well fenced. They are also not known for their road sense so it is as much for their own protection as it is for the safety of other small animals, should they end up at liberty outside your property.

## Very Large Breeds

Very large breeds, or 'giant' breeds, include both tall and heavy dogs, such as Great Danes, Irish Wolfhounds, Mastiffs, Dogue de Bordeaux, Neapolitan Mastiff, and heavily coated dogs like Newfoundlands, Saint Bernards and Bernese Mountain Dogs.

Being large or small has no relationship to the activity level of a breed. There are small breeds with high energy levels and large breeds that are very relaxed. Of course, there are also individuals within any breed that can vary in temperament. Exercise is a requirement of all dogs, regardless of size or breed and although most dogs enjoy a walk and a run at the local park, small breeds like Chihuahuas and other toys can get a reasonable amount of exercise playing and running around a smaller backyard. In contrast, if your yard is too small for a giant breed to be able to move around freely you must be prepared to take your dog out daily to get sufficient exercise to remain fit and healthy, regardless of whether they appear quite content to lie around at home. Most of the giant breeds are very strong so training is particularly important. Their physical size inside a small house can also cause problems. A Great Dane tail can easily clear a table!

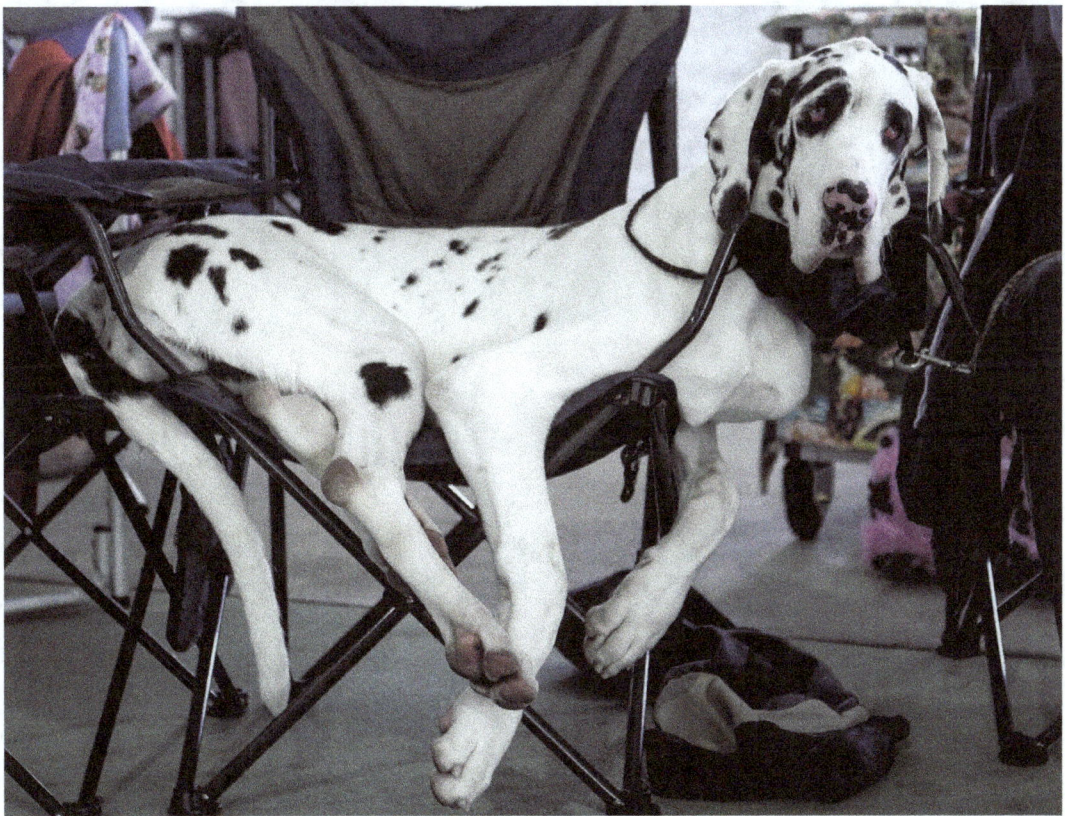

*Giant breeds like Great Danes can be very relaxed and content to lie around but they still require regular exercise to remain healthy.*

Although there are always exceptions, very large breeds such as Great Danes, Newfoundlands, Bernese Mountain Dogs, Saint Bernards and some Mastiff breeds are short lived in comparison to smaller, more athletic breeds. They are also at greater risk of heat stress and some specific health issues such as arthritis and other bone and joint related problems. Gastric dilatation and volvulus (GDV), also known as 'bloat', is a serious life threatening digestive disorder that affects mainly large dogs and breeds with deep chests. Many giant breeds are inclined to drool, so be sure you can cope with this before getting a dog with loose jowls.

*Great Dane*
*Many giant breeds have loose jowls and are therefore inclined to drool.*

Due to the difficulties involved with owning any of the giant breeds, they rarely enter the top ranking of the popularity lists. Bernese Mountain Dogs are the exception in some countries and they are also at the smaller end of the very large breeds. There are many delightful large heavy breeds but it is very important that you be aware of the difficulties associated with owning one. Many giant breed puppies are particularly cute so don't be seduced by appearance alone and choose your breeder carefully. Make sure that it is someone that is well informed, that explains both the positive and negative aspects of the breed you are looking at bringing into your home as a pet.

## Coat

Many of the coat colours, patterns, and textures of domestic dogs bear little resemblance to those of the wolves that they have descended from. A dog's coat and colour contributes to how appealing we find the breed and may influence our choice when choosing a puppy. There is more than aesthetics to consider when choosing a dog though, as many coat types require a great deal of maintenance, and some dogs will shed heavily leaving tumbleweeds of dog hair gathering around the legs of your furniture. When a breed becomes fashionable to own for the wrong reasons, such as being owned by a celebrity, people may ignore the difficulties associated with coat when they choose to buy one, leading to an increase in dogs entering rescues in appalling condition.

*Irish Wolfhounds are one of the breeds that are referred to as 'giant'.*

The genetics of colour inheritance are too complex to address here and colour is not of any great consequence other than to mention that white dogs, particularly if they have no pigment in exposed skin areas like eyes, ears and noses, are more at risk of sun damage and skin cancers and may require sun protection for their skin. Dark dogs are also at a higher risk of heat stress, particularly if they have a heavy coat or a dense undercoat, and some coat colours can be associated with health conditions like 'blue' Dobermanns that tend to suffer from alopecia (hair loss). If you are interested in showing your dog there are colours that are permitted for each breed and some that are not. If you choose a colour that is not recognised in the standard for a breed you will not be able to show your dog.

On the other hand, differences in coat length and texture are predominantly affected by three genes which, in a variety of combinations, are responsible for seven basic coat types. These are the genes for length (long or short haired), wire (wire or non-wire) and curl (straight or curly hair). The wire gene is responsible for producing coarse hair with facial furnishings, the term used by breeders for bushy eyebrows and beards (W = wire) or coats that are not coarse without furnishings (w = non-wire). Combinations include coats that are curly-wire such as the Kerry Blue Terrier, and long and curly such as the Irish Water Spaniel.

*Kerry Blue Terrier (top left) has a curly-wire coat and the Pointer (top right) has a short coat. The Xoloitzcuintle (bottom) can be almost completely hairless.*

Most dog coats grow to a certain length and stop, but in some breeds including Afghans, Maltese, Poodles, Shih Tzu, Pekingese, Schnauzers and Bedlington Terriers the coat grows continuously. Curly coats that grow continuously are capable of forming cords in breeds like the Puli and Komondor, but Poodle coats can also be groomed to cord. There are also hairless breeds like the Chinese Crested and the Xoloitzcuintle. Both of these have a coated version as well. In Chinese Cresteds, the coated variety is referred to as 'Powderpuff' and the coat is long. In Xoloitzcuintle, the coated variety has a short coat.

*The hairless variety of the Chinese Crested dog (left) is without hair except around the head, feet and tail. The coated variety know as 'Powderpuff' (right) has a long flowing coat.*

Coats can also be single or double. Most cold climate breeds like Alaskan Malamutes have dense undercoats (double coats) but other breeds may have undercoats to a lesser degree. Although the amount a dog will shed varies according to breed, and even between individual animals, all dogs will shed to some degree. Dogs with undercoats are likely to shed a great deal more than dogs without an undercoat and will usually replace the undercoat once a year as winter approaches. Some will replace it twice a year in line with the seasons so that they carry a lighter coat in the hotter months. Others shed to a lesser degree but may shed all year, particularly if they are kept inside. Some dog breeds are marketed as hypo-allergenic but there is no guarantee that a dog will not cause an allergic reaction in a family member as a result of the individual's sensitivity to dog saliva or dander. Dog coats can also vary a little according to breed and within the breed itself. A Labrador and a Pointer are both considered short haired breeds but the coat of a Labrador is much longer and thicker than that of a Pointer.

Obviously short coated dogs are the easiest to care for but they should still be washed and brushed regularly. Moderate long coats like Border Collies and Golden Retrievers can be reasonably easy to care for as long as they are brushed regularly enough to prevent tangles and matting. On the other hand, caring for coats that grow continuously can be laborious, or expensive if you intend to pay someone else to care for the coat. Most pet owners choose to have the coat clipped off so that it is more manageable. In this case it is pointless to choose a breed based on the appearance of the dog in full show coat. You should look at what the breed looks like clipped off before deciding on a puppy because this is what you will be living with. To maintain and protect their beautiful coats for the show ring, long coated dogs like Poodles, Shih Tzu and Maltese need to have their coats banded, or wrapped, a technique used by breeders to protect the coat. Sections of the long coat that are most to get soiled are rolled up and tied in lightweight fabric.

Other breeds that are frequently photographed in show coat are Terriers, Schnauzers, Setters, and Cocker Spaniels. The 'look' of these breeds is maintained by stripping excess coat by hand with the fingers, or with stripping tools that are pictured in the grooming section later in the book. It can be very expensive to pay someone to maintain the coat is this manner. Good breeders may demonstrate the technique and help you to master it. Others will again recommend clipping the coat every six to eight weeks. Clipping changes the nature of the coat though, encouraging the soft undercoat to grow through the outer coat, increasing the potential for tangling and matting. The coat also tends to get thicker and curlier after the coat has been clipped a few

*Maltese in full show coat (top). Maltese in two different pet clips (middle and bottom). You should look at what the breed looks like clipped off before deciding on a puppy.*

*Standard poodle in full show clip.*
*This type of clip would be far too much work for most pet owners to maintain.*

times, so it is unlikely that the dog will ever be suited to the show ring after clipping as the correct shape and texture of the coat has been lost.

You might think that the easiest dogs to care for would be the hairless breeds but this would be wrong. They actually require more work than breeds with short coats due to the fact that, without hair to protect them, their skin requires more care. They tend to require weekly baths, skin moisturizers and protection from the sun in the form of light 'sun' coats or sunscreen. Of course, they are also inclined to feel the cold so they will need to wear coats as well if the weather is cool.

Coats that are not maintained will become matted and dirty, increasing dog odours and the likelihood of skin conditions, embedded grass seeds, and infestations from parasites and fly larvae. These conditions will obviously cause your dog considerable discomfort so make sure that you have the time and inclination, or the financial resources, to adequately care for the coat of a breed you may be interested in.

*Miniature Schnauzer*
*The show coat is maintained by hand stripping. Clipping is recommended for pets but it alters the appearance of the coat.*

## Temperament

There is nothing more devastating than finding out that the puppy you have brought into your home has a temperament problem. To what extent the temperament problem is an issue often relates to your personal circumstances. A dog that is timid when out in public, but confident and happy at home, may not be too much of a problem if the dog is a pet. If you want a dog to accompany you to other places, to compete in dog sports, the show ring, or participate in other social activities, being timid is something that is definitely undesirable. In addition, you would not want to expose children to an aggressive dog, but a timid dog may also be inclined to snap defensively at your children from fear.

The difficulty with temperament problems is that they may be acquired, rather than genetic due to the way the animal has been raised or treated in the past. Poorly socialised dogs or dogs that have experienced trauma or abuse can be timid. Socialised from an early age with people and other dogs, the same dog could be outgoing, friendly and confident. Aggression may also be a learned response but both aggression and timidity can be genetic.

Breeders may refer to dogs as having a 'soft' temperament. This is different from being timid. Dogs with soft temperaments can be the best family dogs. They are often gentle and friendly but are easily upset by harsh treatment. A dog with a soft temperament could easily become timid as a learned response if treated badly.

For a family dog, a bold outgoing personality is probably best as they may be more tolerant of children and loud noise. Hyperactive dogs with high energy levels or a strong working drive may be too much to deal with in a family situation. You need to take particular care when selecting dogs from breeds that are still used in working roles. For instance, working line German Shepherds that are still used by the police and the military are chosen for their strong working drive. Although these dogs adapt extremely well to training, they are likely to be too active for family life.

Temperament varies between individual breeds, dogs within a breed, and even within litters. This is the major problem with breed specific legislation that targets a whole breed based on dogs that are often the result of poor breeding, poor socialisation and a lack of, or incorrect, training. It is irresponsible and ignorant to suggest that an entire breed has a dangerous temperament. There are many good breeders that work hard to ensure that the temperament of their dogs is good. With socialisation, training, and proper supervision, these breeds can be fine.

*With socialisation, training, and proper supervision, well bred breeds that are frequently targeted by breed specific legislation (BSL) can be fine.*

It would be almost impossible to give a description of temperaments that are associated with, or desirable for, each breed group. As mentioned earlier, some breed groups have a great deal of variation within them, particularly in the non-sporting group where breeds vary from Poodles to Bulldogs. The temperament of some toy breeds can be reserved and shy while others like the Maltese should be outgoing. Some generalisations can be made that relate to the breed's history and purpose. Terriers and Gundogs, like Labradors, Pointers and other Retrievers should be confident and outgoing, never timid, due to the fact that the breeds were developed to accompany hunters. It is best to familiarise yourself with the breed standard as this describes the desirable temperament for the breed. Talk to breed clubs and as many breeders as you can before looking at puppies. It can be very difficult to determine the temperament when choosing a puppy so it is important to look at the temperament of the parents if at all possible. Often, the tendency to be timid, hyperactive or aggressive comes later. There are guidelines later in the book in 'Selecting a Healthy Puppy' page 59 that may help you.

*Terriers should be confident and outgoing.*

*Some toy breeds can be reserved but others like the Maltese should be outgoing.*

## Health

Just as humans can suffer from a multitude of ailments, dogs are also at risk of developing a range of health issues. Common canine health issues which can affect any dog, regardless of breed are discussed later in this book. There are also many canine health issues and diseases that are genetic in origin. Purebred dog breeders have been widely criticised as causing these conditions to become more prevalent through selective breeding and inbreeding. While this may have been the case in the past, it should also be pointed out that many genetic diseases are a problem for more than one breed. As a result, mixed breeds are not automatically immune to developing a genetic problem. For instance, several large breeds are prone to hip dysplasia including Labradors and Poodles. Labradoodles, Labradors crossed with Poodles, are therefore also at risk of developing hip dysplasia but the incidence of the problem in purebred dogs can be minimized by careful breeding and screening.

With the advent of DNA testing, many of these genetic health issues can now be identified in both dogs that suffer from the disease, and dogs that carry the gene for the disease and whose future offspring may therefore suffer from the disease. Modes of genetic inheritance are covered later in 'Common Health Issues' (page 153) but what is important to know at this stage is that responsible breeders of purebred dogs are working to eliminate these diseases from their breed by using health testing to remove affected dogs from their breeding programs. The testing is expensive and therefore most backyard breeders are unlikely to bother so you should be wary of purchasing puppies from unregistered breeders and untested parents.

Some breeds, including some of the most popular breeds, potentially suffer from more genetic disorders than others. The English Bulldog and the French Bulldog are very popular in some countries and many people are aware that these breeds are at risk of numerous genetic disorders based on their physical appearance, such as skeletal problems and the fact that they are a brachycephalic breed. In contrast, people are less likely to be aware that other popular breeds like Golden Retrievers and German Shepherd Dogs are also at risk of quite a few genetic disorders. Some genetic problems are considered at high risk for a breed and others may be low risk, occurring only occasionally. It is highly recommended that you research the breed that you are interested in to identify potential health problems and the level of risk to the breed of each disorder. You should also consider the consequences of your dog developing one of these problems and whether you can meet the expense of treating this disorder. For instance, a large percentage of Chinese Shar Pei require surgery to correct entropion, eyelashes that turn inward and irritate the eyes. While the incidence of entropion is reducing through the efforts of good breeders, and the surgery is generally successful, you should

*French Bulldog, a brachycephalic (short nosed) breed with potential for other genetic disorders.*

*German Shepherd Dogs bred by good breeders from health tested parents can be very sound but others can suffer from a number of genetic disorders.*

still be prepared for the consequences of entropion if you choose to buy a Shar Pei puppy. This does not mean that you should never consider getting a breed that has a high incidence of genetic disorders, but you should be careful in the choice of your breeder and be aware of what to expect if the dog does develop the condition in future.

Although there are many different diseases and disorders, common genetic issues include muscular and skeletal problems, eye disorders, heart and circulatory conditions, and skin conditions. The most common skeletal disorders include hip and elbow dysplasia, luxating patella and growth related bone disorders like panosteitis. Skeletal problems are more likely to affect larger more active breeds and large mixed breeds as well. Conditions such as hip and elbow dysplasia can also be affected by poor diet and excessive and potentially damaging exercise during a puppy's rapid growth period such as

*The Chinese Shar Pei may suffer from entropion that requires surgery to correct.*

jumping. Common eye problems include progressive retinal atrophy (PRA), cataracts, entropion and ectropion, a condition where the lower eyelid turns outwards so the inner surface is exposed.

By far the best way to avoid purchasing a puppy with the potential for genetic disease is to support responsible breeders who breed selectively with health tested dogs and who are prepared to guarantee the health of their puppies. It may be more expensive initially but it may save you a lot of medical expense and heartache later on. More detail on these genetic disorders and others that may affect breeds that you are interested in can be found on our website at http://www.animalinfo.com.au.

## Rare Breeds

There are a number of dog breeds that are considered rare. These breeds have become rare due to the fact that they have fallen out of favour or they are no longer required to do the work for which they were originally bred. So why include them in a chapter on popular breeds? Sometimes their unique and unusual appearance makes them appealing and the attention that they attract can lead to a revival in the popularity of the breed.

Owning a rare breed though, can require more dedication than owning a common breed. With some of the breeds nearing extinction, the gene pool is often very small leading to an increase in health and temperament problems, though some rare breeds like the Xoloitzcuintle and the Azawakh are surprisingly sound. In addition, breeds like the Xoloitzcuintle are classified as 'primitive' breeds. Primitive breeds are less likely to respond to people who they do not know well so their temperament may not appeal to everyone.

*Xoloitzcuintle are classified as a 'primitive' breed. Primitive breeds are less likely to respond to people who they do not know well.*

There are often very dedicated breeders associated with the rare breeds and it is important to seek those out if you are looking at obtaining a rare breed. There is often a waiting list for puppies but it is well worth the wait to get a puppy from someone that is experienced and knowledgeable about the breed.

*Eight month old Tibetan Mastiff, also a rare breed. These are an ancient giant breed originally used to guard flocks in Tibet.*

*Azawakh, an ancient breed originating in Africa.
Azawakh are surprisingly sound even though they are considered a rare breed.*

*Irish Red and White Setter.*
*This breed became almost extinct in the early 1900s after the Irish Red Setter gained popularity.*

# Finding Your New Dog

*Papillon*

## Breeders of Purebred Dogs

Purebred dogs are bred and exhibited all over the world. Dog shows are generally administered by Kennel Clubs and Societies. Along with administering the shows these bodies also provide breed standards and lists of breeders that are registered with them. They may not inspect kennels to ascertain whether the registered breeders are caring for their dogs properly, so purchasing from a registered breeder does not guarantee the health of a dog. They do impose rules and guidelines for ethical breeding and are able to impose fines, for example, fining breeders for breeding with dogs that are too young. Dogs are expected to be presented for exhibition in excellent condition though registered breeders are not obliged to show their dogs.

The major Societies have websites and can be contacted by email or phone. Due to the large number of members that they have they will not recommend a specific breeder but can generally advise you on show dates where you can see and speak with breeders who are exhibiting on the day. They often have lists on their website of registered breeders, but you should be aware that these are not breeders that they recommend, but breeders who have paid for the privilege of advertising on the Society's website. Breeders also advertise in the many dog magazines that are distributed around the world.

*Dogs are expected to be presented for judging in excellent condition.*

Genuine breeders incur many costs in producing their puppies such as veterinary fees for the mother prior to mating, stud fees, litter and puppy registration fees, in addition to large food bills and the expense of worming, vaccinations and vet checks for the pups prior to sale. A lactating bitch will need to increase her food intake dramatically to produce enough milk to feed her growing litter without losing condition herself. Many bitches that produce litters as a result of uncontrolled breeding, by owners that have little or no knowledge of breeding, will end up extremely thin and weak as a result of feeding their pups. In many cases a responsible breeder will also have incurred the costs of DNA testing of their breeding stock to eliminate genetic faults and diseases from their line. As a result of these costs, it is reasonable to expect to pay more for a pedigree pup from a good breeder even if the pup is not a potential show champion. It is also reasonable to expect to pay a higher price for a pup that is likely to be competitive in the show ring. It is important to know that puppies can change dramatically as they grow, so no breeder can guarantee that your puppy will be a champion. Sometimes the least promising puppy can grow into the best dog in the litter and the best will go the other way, particularly if the new owner does not provide the correct diet and health care to maximise the pup's growth and development.

*A purebred American Staffordshire Terrier with her litter. Both mother and pups are in excellent condition due to the diet and care of the breeder.*

It is best to try and locate a number of breeders so that you can get some different perspectives on the breed you are contemplating buying. Breeders may contradict each other which may indicate that more research on a particular aspect of the breed is in order. It is important to look at how a breeder relates to their dogs, and to you. A good breeder will be interested in how their dog develops and will be looking for owners who will provide a good home for the life of the dog. Choose a breeder that

*Chihuahua Puppy*
*It is reasonable to expect to pay a higher price for a pup that may be competitive in the show ring.*

you can build a rapport with. They should be happy to help you if you have any concerns about the health and development of your dog. Good breeders will often have waiting lists for their puppies and may not need to advertise for business.

*It is important to look at how a breeder relates to their dogs.*

After deciding on the breed of dog you wish to own it can be helpful to approach breed specific clubs. These clubs will often have social events or training days where you can speak with members. Although there will be breeders amongst the members, there will also be many owners who can recommend or warn against breeders they have dealt with. Breeders who provide good service and have a good reputation will come highly recommended. In addition some clubs have instigated breed surveys and tests that breeding animals are required to pass. These tests are designed to improve the health and temperament of the breed. Most breed clubs can be located through the major Kennel Councils.

Links to the major worldwide Kennel Councils are provided in the 'Resources' chapter (page 167).

## Pet Shops

Like most things there are good and bad pet shops, but the biggest problem with all pet shops is that they cater for the impulse buyer who falls in love with a puppy that they have seen in a shop window. The notion of researching the breed, being realistic about their personal situation and everything else I have already mentioned goes out the window. Many dogs, and owners, who start their relationship under these circumstances, also end their relationship at the door to a rescue shelter.

People can sometimes feel compelled to 'save' puppies from some of the conditions in bad pet shops. While this is understandable, it also creates a market that supports shops that do not care for their puppies properly. If you want to save a puppy or dog, consider giving a dog from a rescue organisation or shelter a home.

*French Bulldog Puppy*
*In most countries you can purchase a purebred pup from a pet shop but not one with pedigree papers.*

If you are happy to purchase a pup from a pet shop you should still be clear on what you are looking for before going shopping to avoid buying a dog that will become a problem. You should have a clear idea of whether you want a large or small dog and some general research into common breeds is a good idea. Many crossbred pups that are offered by pet shops are combinations of some of the most common breeds. However, the genetic origin of many pups may be misrepresented simply because the owner of the shop does not know the background of the puppies. For example, they may be crosses from crosses, so there is no longer any distinct breed characteristics left to distinguish.

In most countries you may be able to purchase a purebred pup from a pet shop but not one with pedigree papers, as most kennel councils do not permit the sale of registered pups to pet shops. It is considered the responsibility of ethical, genuine breeders to organise the sale of their own dogs and puppies. It is largely this fact that has led to an upsurge in the development of 'designer' breeds that command a higher price, and therefore, a better financial return for shop owners without having to supply the paperwork to justify the additional costs.

Many pet shops turn over large numbers of puppies. The environment of a pet shop can also be very stressful for young puppies. The hygiene of the shop is extremely important to prevent the outbreak of disease and it is also essential that the puppy is wormed and fully vaccinated. There is nothing more heartbreaking than watching a puppy die from a preventable disease. A pet shop must be exceptionally clean and provide proof that the pups have had the necessary vaccinations. Because of the young age of many pups in pet shops, most will only have had their first vaccination. This means that they are still vulnerable to infection until after they have had their second vaccination at ten to twelve weeks.

## Rescue Shelters

Far too many dogs eventually find themselves in rescue shelters – the result of uncontrolled breeding, poorly considered choice, abuse, neglect, and sometimes due to the death or relocation of the owner. Many people are under the misguided notion that their dog's life will not be fulfilled if it does not have the opportunity to breed. In reality this is more likely to be an excuse that people use to justify allowing their dog to breed so they themselves can enjoy the experience of having a litter of cute puppies for a while. Many people do not get their dogs sterilised because they don't wish to incur the cost, but do not have adequate fencing to ensure that unwanted litters don't result. The world has far too many dogs so unless you have a strongly justifiable reason for breeding you should ensure that you budget for having your dog or bitch sterilised. If you are still deciding whether to allow your dog to breed, a trip to the nearest animal rescue shelter may just be the reality check you require. Their statistics on euthanasia of dogs that cannot be re-homed can be quite shocking.

There are several different types of rescue facilities. The RSPCA (Royal Society for the Prevention of Cruelty to Animals) began in Wales and England in 1824. This largely voluntary organisation has spread throughout the world and spawned other similar organisations most of which have SPCA (Society for the Prevention of Cruelty to Animals) as part of their titles. These organisations investigate many alleged cases of neglect and abuse each year and re-home tens of thousands of dogs. Links to the main organisations in this group around the world are listed below.

- http://www.rspca.org.au/ in Australia
- http://www.rspca.org.uk in United Kingdom
- http://rnzspca.org.nz/ in New Zealand
- http://www.aspca.org in the USA

There are also many smaller privately funded organisations run by volunteers that do an excellent job and deserve to be supported. You can find the nearest rescue centre by using your telephone directory, the internet, or even contacting the main SPCA in your country that may be able to recommend the nearest reputable shelter. It is best to do some research on the internet or perhaps with the local council or county to check on the reputation of the organisation offering to re-home dogs.

There are also breed specific rescues so even if you are considering a purebred you may still be able to offer a good home to a dog that needs it. One of the benefits of this type of shelter is that the rescue volunteers are usually people that have a lot of experience with the breed and therefore can be both realistic and

*Great Dane rescue dog 'Annie'*

helpful about the suitability of the breed for your personal circumstances. The fact that a dog was unsuitable for one situation does not mean that it wouldn't be perfect for someone else.

By choosing an adult dog you can often avoid some of the household destruction that comes with puppyhood. On the other hand, some animals at shelters will never have had any training or attention and will therefore behave badly and require even more work than a puppy to become a good companion. Others may have been permanently scarred by the abuse that they have received at the hands of their previous owners and will require a great deal of patience, care and attention to overcome their mistrust of humans. A good shelter does not want to see the dogs returned and will screen new owners thoroughly to assess whether the dog is suitable. Dogs from shelters are not free! It costs a great deal of money to care for these animals and they will usually sterilise the animal and make sure that it is parasite free and vaccinated before being re-homed. These are the things that a responsible dog owner should be prepared to pay for! The links provided below supply many of the breed rescue groups located around the world.

- http://www.animalinfo.com.au worldwide
- http://www.dogrescueusa.com/ in USA
- http://www.dogzonline.com.au in Australia
- http://www.dogzonline.co.uk in United Kingdom

*The fact that a dog was unsuitable for one situation does not mean that it wouldn't be perfect for someone else.*

*Griffon Bruxellois Puppy*
*Good breeders will often have waiting lists for their puppies.*

*Beagle Puppy*
*Healthy pups can be purchased from responsible breeders who care for their dogs well.*

# Selecting a Healthy Puppy

*Staffordshire Bull Terrier Puppy*

## What Should You Expect From a Supplier?

In the case of rescue shelters and pet shops, the supplier can probably only provide you with limited information on a particular animal, other than outlining the health checks and procedures that they have carried out while the dog was in their care. Occasionally they have more history on an animal depending on the circumstances which brought it to the shop or shelter, but any genetic health information is usually not available. You should still receive proof of vaccination before accepting a dog or puppy.

On the other hand if you are purchasing a purebred puppy from a registered breeder there is a great deal more information that can and should be supplied. A good breeder's premises should be clean and not smell too strongly. For quarantine and noise reasons (many dogs will bark vigorously when people enter the kennels), they may not wish to give you a full tour and should not be expected to, but if you are considering purchasing a puppy they should at least allow you to see the whole litter, the mother of the pups and her pedigree papers. If the father is their dog you should be able to see him also, but if an outside stud was used then this may not be possible, however it would be good to see a photo. If you are considering buying a puppy with pedigree papers, then you should also be shown the sire's

*It is important to see the mother of the pups as this will be the best indicator of the final appearance and temperament of the puppies.*

papers and his show records. It is important to see the sire and dam as this is the best indication you will get as to the potential personality and physical appearance of the pups when they are fully grown. If a pup is being offered as purebred, but either the sire or dam is unregistered, there is no guarantee of genetic purity.

The breeder's dogs should be in good condition or there should be a good explanation for any dogs that aren't. Adult dogs moult twice a year and many medium to long coated dogs can look a bit dull and moth eaten at this time, but the dog should still have good body condition, bright eyes and appear happy and active at the prospect of attention.

*Pugs*
*Other dogs belonging to the breeder should be in good condition.*

A good breeder should be aware of any genetic disorders that the breed suffers from and will have had their breeders tested if possible. Some genetic tests are not readily available all over the world, so if the breeder has not had the opportunity to test their dogs, they should at least make you aware of this fact and that the disorder may be a problem with the breed. A breeder who is unaware of the disorders that are a potential problem in their breed should be avoided. They are either not a good breeder or they may be trying to deceive you. There are many websites that will list and describe the disorders that are a potential problem for each breed. You will find some listed in the 'Resources' section at the end of this book.

You should ask about the worming regime that they use for their puppies. Good breeders will be aware that puppies should be wormed fortnightly from two weeks of age with a special puppy wormer until they are twelve weeks of age, at which time the worming treatments become less frequent. A small puppy that has carried a worm burden will not be as well developed as it should be. You should also enquire as to the diet the puppies have been on, however a good breeder should make you aware of this without being asked, as sudden changes in diet can cause diarrhoea and they would not want this to happen.

## Veterinary Certification

As mentioned earlier, sellers should supply new owners with proof of any vaccinations that the puppies have had. Vaccination protocols vary from country to country and even between states within some countries, so it is best to contact a local vet before purchasing a pup. They will advise you on what vaccinations puppies should have, relevant to the area you live in and at what age these should be given. The owner should provide a certificate that has been signed by the veterinarian administering the vaccination, and include the vet's contact details. It should also state the type of vaccine, the date of administration and recommendations for when the next booster is due. Vets issue one certificate per pup injected, and they should include some relevant details on the pup such as age, breed, colour and sex. Unfortunately, unless a pup is micro-chipped, these certificates don't include any more specific identification details.

*Puppies require regular worming from two weeks of age.*

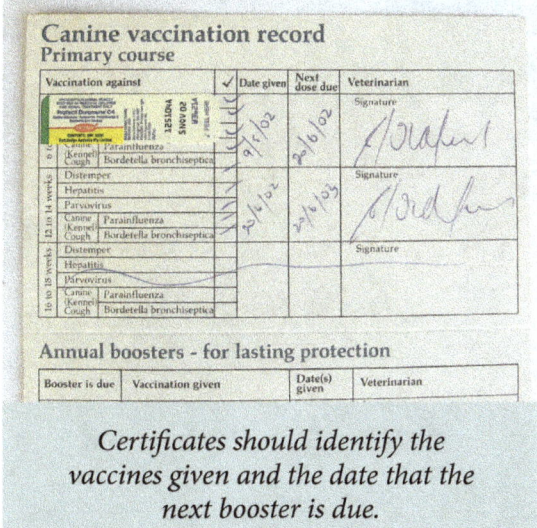

*Certificates should identify the vaccines given and the date that the next booster is due.*

Some owners will advertise that their puppies have been vet checked as well as vaccinated. While it is true that most vets will perform a basic health check prior to vaccination, the certificate is proof of vaccination only. A vet may identify a health problem with a puppy but the breeder may not choose to pass the information onto the new owner. Unless you receive a written veterinary report that clearly outlines the checks performed by a veterinary practice, you cannot assume that a puppy has been certified as being healthy.

## Pedigree Papers and Contracts

If a breeder registers a litter with their governing kennel club, council or society, the puppies will have papers that supply details of their breeder, colour, date of birth, registration number, official or 'show' name, and the dog's pedigree. This usually tracks the dog's parentage for around three generations and includes the championship status of all the dogs in their pedigree, including any obedience or sporting titles they may have gained.

Even pups born to champion parents may not all be potential champions. Some may carry conformation, colour or marking faults, be too small or too large, may have slightly incorrect teeth alignment or some other undesirable fault making them unsuitable for breeding or show purposes. These are still fine for someone wanting a companion dog for themselves or their family. If the faults are obvious when the pup is young, a breeder may only offer the pup for sale without their papers, or with a non-breeding contract that obliges the new owner to sterilise the puppy at the appropriate time.

Some kennel clubs allow breeders to register their pups on a 'limited register'. In this case, the dog is sold with pedigree papers but it cannot be shown, and any pups produced from the dog cannot be registered. If you choose the best pup in the litter the breeder may refuse to sell it without papers and they have a right to do so. If you are only looking for a non-breeding pet then make the breeder aware so they can indicate which puppies you should choose from. Some research on your part, prior to visiting a kennel, will help you be aware of what points are considered major show faults. However, a good breeder with experience should be prepared to point out the faults in the pups you are viewing and explain why they are considered to be non-breeding or showing dogs. Pups without pedigree papers, or with 'limited register' papers, may be less expensive than those sold with full papers and pups with serious faults, such as overbites, should never be supplied with full 'breeding and showing' pedigree papers under any circumstances.

*Regardless of how promising they may appear, it is impossible to predict whether a puppy with potential, like this Jack Russell Terrier, will grow into a show quality adult.*

If you are purchasing a puppy with papers you will generally be required to fill out your details on the transfer section of the pedigree papers. The pedigree papers will then be sent to you by the respective kennel councils that have issued the original papers and when they arrive they will have your name on them. Ensure that you get a copy of the transfer that you have filled in and a receipt that indicates you have paid for a registered pedigree pup so that if the papers do not arrive when they should you have some proof that you are entitled to receive them. If the pup has had any genetic or medical examinations for things like hearing defects or hip dysplasia, make sure you receive a copy of the test results as well as their vaccination certificates. If the breeder has advertised the fact that the parents have had genetic testing, you are entitled to sight copies of the test results.

Some breeders may require new owners to sign contracts which outline the conditions of sale and any non-breeding or showing clauses that they require the new owner to abide by. They differ from breeder to breeder so the only advice I can give is that you ask for a copy of the contract in advance and make sure that you read it thoroughly and are happy with the conditions before signing it and collecting the puppy. A good breeder will care about where their puppies are going to end up so be prepared to answer their questions honestly. They know the breed better than you do so they may save you from making a serious mistake.

## Available Health Screening

It is important to note that genetic diseases are not specific to purebred dogs. All dogs are susceptible to genetic disease but the tracking of pedigrees, genetic testing and controlled breeding practised by good breeders provides an opportunity to reduce the incidence of these diseases in future generations.

Many genetic disorders won't be obvious in a young puppy, and in fact sometimes won't become noticeable until they become adults. Therefore, the best way to get some idea of whether a puppy may inherit a health problem is to look at the disease status of the parents. Responsible breeders will generally only breed from stock that has been certified clear of diseases that they could possibly pass on to their offspring. These test results may also be added to a health database, which in some cases is accessible to the general public. The value of these databases is that they allow responsible breeders to select stock that will improve the health of the breed, while putting pressure on less responsible breeders by giving prospective puppy purchasers the ability to recognise a breeder with documented good genetic lines. The popular use of databases varies from country to country, and failure to use them by breeders does not necessarily mean that the quality of the breeder

*Cavalier King Charles Spaniel Puppy
Many genetic disorders won't be obvious in a young puppy.*

and their stock is questionable. There are a number of easily accessible health registries, particularly in America, where, given the pedigree name of the animal, anyone can look up test results and disease status (see the 'Resources' chapter at the end of the book for registries).

*Great Dane Puppy*
*Health testing, such as heart testing for Great Danes, is becoming common place as a result of breeders efforts to improve the health of their breed.*

Breeders with poor test results are not obliged to make the information available but many do. Those with good results will often be happy to add them to a database as it helps advertise the fact that their dogs are free of genetic diseases. If you find a breeder you may be interested in talking to about obtaining a puppy, and a health database is accessible in your country, why not find out the names of some of their dogs and check on their health status yourself?

New health tests are regularly coming on to the market, generally as a result of demand from breeders to constantly improve the health of their breed, and I would encourage potential buyers to take advantage of these new preventative health techniques. However, screening of the parents of a prospective new puppy, should be proportional to the seriousness and prevalence of each potential disease within that breed, otherwise testing for every possibility could get out of hand and cost thousands of dollars unnecessarily. The extent to which health screening is recommended when purchasing a dog varies between countries, kennel clubs, breeds and personal preference. For example, the Kennel Club of Great Britain has a list of tests for each breed that must be carried out on the sire and dam of a litter, before that litter can even be eligible for registration. In other countries, the major breed clubs or councils will also often make similar recommendations for health testing, and it is worth contacting these associations before talking to breeders about obtaining a puppy, so you know what health issues are regionally important for your breed. Some genetic disorders occur only rarely in a breed or only in specific lines. Discuss these diseases with breeders anyway, and if you have any doubts about the soundness of their stock, ask about the possibility of a screening test.

If you take a little time to be as sure about the future health of your dog as possible, you will undoubtedly save yourself a lot more time and expense later on, you and your dog will have much more fun together, and you will be encouraging the responsible breeding of healthy dogs for future generations.

*By being a discerning buyer you will be encouraging responsible breeding of healthy dogs for future generations.*

## Visual Examination

If you are considering purchasing a purebred puppy, it is best to do your homework on potential suppliers before going to look at litters. Puppies are so difficult to resist, even if they don't appear perfectly healthy or as well developed as they should be for their age. If you identify breeders beforehand, you will have the opportunity to visit a number of them and decide on which line of breeding you prefer in areas such as temperament and conformation, colour and markings. In addition, you can get an idea of how well they care for their dogs, how clean their establishment and their adult dogs are, and how ethical they are in their breeding activities. They also have the opportunity to ask questions of you as a potential buyer, and may even advise you that the breed is not suitable for your living arrangements or your family situation. I once witnessed a young couple contemplating the spontaneous purchase of a Bull Mastiff /Staffordshire Bull Terrier cross in a pet shop for their two year old daughter- a recipe for disaster! By the time it was four months old, this cross would be likely to be far too heavy and far too active for a small child.

If you can be patient, it's better to order and wait for a pup from a breeder that has clean healthy dogs, than to choose a pup from the first establishment that you visit. Once you're confronted with a litter at a shop or at a purebred kennel, whether the purchase was planned in advance or not, there are a number of things to look for in selecting a healthy happy puppy.

Puppies should be clean and not smell bad. They defecate

*French Bulldog Puppies*
*Puppies are so difficult to resist, it is best to identify good breeders before going to look at litters.*

often, and as they are always rolling around playing they can end up having sat or rolled in something that they shouldn't have. However, a healthy puppy with a good coat is extremely dirt resistant. If they have been kept in a clean environment they shouldn't have a grubby dull appearance. If they do, this would indicate a poor diet, poor housing and probably internal and external parasites.

Unless you have seen them eat a full meal, puppies should not have round, pot bellies. This is often mistaken for being fat but it is usually a sign of a puppy that has a heavy worm burden, particularly if it is tight, like tapping a drum. They will often have associated poor bone development, and although their belly is round, their vertebrae may stick up in the centre of their back. It is estimated that 70% of all puppies are born infested with Toxocara canis (roundworm), which have been contracted from the mother in the womb. The pups may also ingest eggs in their mother's milk and from her faeces. Worming should begin at two weeks of age and continue at two weekly intervals until they are twelve weeks of age. Although you may get rid of an infested puppy's worms once you take it home, you can never correct the damage that has been done to their development in these early stages.

*Pups should have good coats and exhibit strong bone development. Unless you have seen them eat a full meal, puppies should not have round pot bellies.*

Puppies should be free from external parasites. There is no excuse for puppies carrying fleas or any other form of parasite. Fleas are the most common infestation that dogs will have, and are the easiest to identify. Most puppies are only too happy to roll on their backs for a tummy rub and this is one of the areas where it is easy to spot fleas. You can also part the hair around the lower back area. A mild infestation of fleas may not have caused the puppies any long term damage (unless they are allergic to flea saliva, causing skin infections), but it is a reflection on the quality of the establishment offering the pups for sale. Pups with fleas are more likely to have worms because fleas act as hosts in the life cycle of some worms. Dogs can also carry lice and mites, which although less common, can cause skin disorders. Ticks and their larvae are also less common but are associated with some serious canine diseases. It is best to have a good look at all areas of exposed skin, avoiding pups that have any signs of skin irritations. You should also run your fingers thoroughly through their coat, looking and feeling for any lumps or things that you can feel crawling.

*Most puppies are only too happy to roll on their backs for a tummy rub and this is one of the areas where it is easy to spot fleas.*

Check the eyes and ears of the puppies. They should be free from any discharge and their ears should not have a bad odour. This may be a sign of ear mites or an ear infection. Some breeds have deafness in their genetic background and this can be difficult to pick up in a group of pups. Deaf puppies quickly learn to use the behaviour of litter mates as a visual cue as to when to look up or come in response to an audible cue that the others have heard. When you have decided on a pup, ask to take it into an area away from the other pups and any other dogs, and then try and see if you get a response from sounds made out of the visual range of the puppy. This is particularly important in breeds that have genetic deafness as a common fault such as Dalmatians or Australian Cattle Dogs which have Dalmatian in their background.

*Check the eyes and ears of the puppies. They should be free from any discharge and their ears should not have a bad odour.*

The coat of a puppy is usually soft and loose and should be fairly shiny. Look around at the puppies' droppings. If they are eating solid food and they are healthy, the droppings should be well formed.

Pups should not have diarrhoea. A soiled bottom could be a sign of this and may be the result of worms as discussed earlier, or disease and bacterial infections. Pups will often get diarrhoea as a result of a change of diet and the stress of a new environment, but it shouldn't happen until after you have taken the puppy home.

In a way puppies are like battery operated toys. They need to recharge often so they sleep frequently. When they first wake up and shake off the sleepiness, they are fully charged and should be bright, active and playful until their batteries run low and they fall asleep again. Avoid pups that are listless and uninterested in their litter mates and things going on around them. Watching the way they play and interact with their litter mates is a good indication of temperament as well. You will be able to spot the dominant dogs that may be potentially dog-aggressive in future, though it is not

*The coat of a puppy is usually soft and loose and should be fairly shiny.*

*Puppies need to sleep frequently but should be bright and active once awake.*

unusual for there to be sounds of growling and snapping as part of normal puppy play. Shy pups may simply be the result of a litter that has not been well socialised, but it may also be a sign of a timid dog. This may not bother you, but if you wish to show, this may present a problem in the future as very timid dogs may not show well. Timid pups may also become fear aggressive without proper socialisation, a problem that is often made worse by owners reassuring them, and therefore reinforcing the behaviour. It is important to get advice early from a good trainer or behaviourist if you decide on a timid puppy.

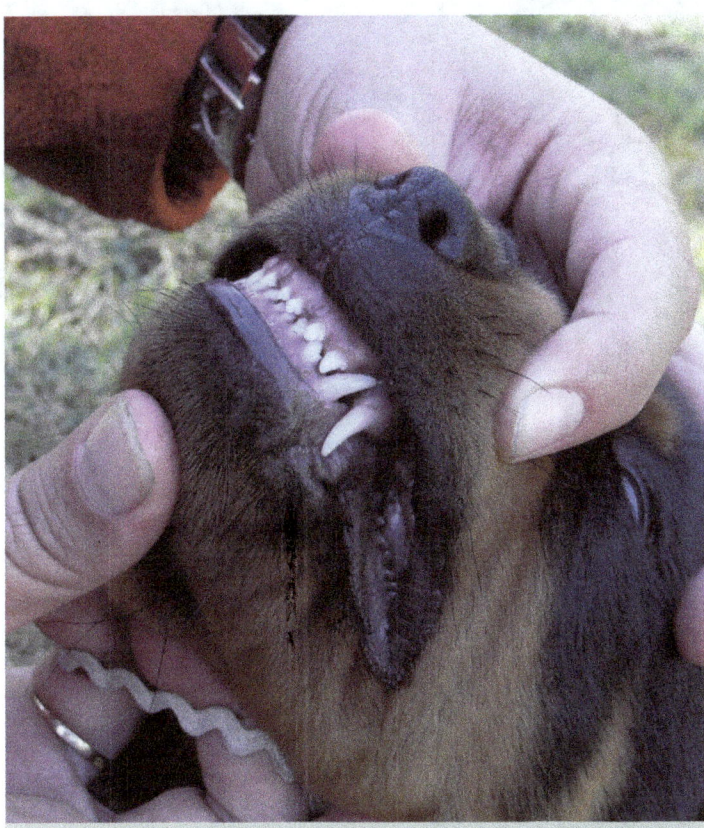

*Look at the pup's teeth alignment. With many breeds, an incorrect bite can be a serious show fault but it can also require expensive dental procedures in a pet.*

Look inside the pup's mouth at the teeth alignment. With many breeds, an incorrect bite can be a serious show fault, but it also has potential health issues in severe cases. Dogs with incorrect teeth alignment may require expensive dental work in order to prevent painful mouth problems caused by misaligned fangs penetrating the gums.

Undescended testicles can be a problem with male puppies and unfortunately they do not usually descend until the pup is older. If you are purchasing a show or breeding animal you should ask the breeder what their policy is on the return of a pup that does not end up with two descended testicles. Although this dog will probably still be fertile, he will not be permitted to show or father registered puppies. It is not an issue for a male pet dog that should be neutered anyway, but the operation to remove an undescended testicle that is located further up in the abdomen is more involved and therefore costlier than the normal procedure. A dog with a retained testicle is also considered to be at higher risk of health complications as they get older if the testicle is not removed. If they are located in the correct position, an experienced vet or breeder can often feel the presence of both testicles before they descend but this is no guarantee that they will drop at the appropriate time.

In reality puppies often choose their owners despite our best efforts to be logical and objective about our decision, but it is best to try and be realistic in your choice, as the wrong decision can be devastating and costly in the long run.

*In reality puppies often choose their owners despite our best efforts to be logical and objective about our decision.*

# Bringing Your Puppy Home

White German Shepherd Puppy

## Preparing For Your New Puppy

If you have thought long and hard about your decision to get a puppy, you have the advantage of being able to prepare your home for the new arrival. The first thing that you need to do is organise some time off work, or at the very least, make sure that you arrange to collect the pup early in the day on a weekend.

All pups are different. Some take everything in their stride with minimum stress while others become very anxious at any changes in their circumstances. This can apply to littermates, not just different breeds so it is best to assume your new pup will be upset by being taken to strange new surroundings after being separated from its mother and littermates. Leaving a pup alone will only exacerbate this anxiety, whereas providing support and comfort during this time will definitely help to form a bond between you and your new dog. While you might want to show off your new puppy, too many people and too much noise can cause a pup to become stressed and this can quickly lead to illness. The only social engagement for the first day or so should be limited to your veterinarian. Unless you have complete confidence in the breeder, a quick trip to the vet on the way home for a physical check up is a good idea.

*It is reasonable to expect your pup to be upset after being separated from its mother and the rest of the litter.*

There are things that you can do to help to make the transition to your home less stressful. Make sure you have acquired anything

that you will need for the pup in advance. This includes suitable food and water containers, bedding, and some toys that are appropriate for the pup's size and age. If you take a small blanket with you to the breeder, the blanket can be rubbed on the mother to collect some of her scent. Having this to sleep on can have a reassuring affect on the puppy.

Sudden changes in the pup's diet can cause diarrhoea. If you have pre-ordered a pup from a breeder it should be easy to obtain details of their diet beforehand, to ensure that you have the right food available. Otherwise, you should try and obtain the same food on the way home. The pup will also be more likely to eat if the food is familiar. If you are unable to obtain the same food, choose a good quality processed puppy food, rather than relying on the pup to eat adult dog food, raw meat or human scraps, as these are likely to upset the pup's digestive system. Puppies need to eat more often than adult dogs, which is one of the reasons that it is best to be at home with a new pup. A normal eight hour working day is too long for a very young pup to wait for a meal. Food should be left for the pup to access if you are going to be away for a full day but this is not ideal as the food may spoil before you get home.

*It is best to obtain details of the pup's diet from the breeder in order to avoid diarrhoea.*

You need to know where the puppy is going to sleep. Consistency is extremely important with dogs. Most dog owners like their dogs to share their home. In temperate climates, others prefer that their dogs remain outside. If you don't intend to allow your dog to be in the house, then don't begin by allowing the pup to sleep inside. Forcing it outside after it has become accustomed to sleeping inside will be confusing for the puppy. If the pup is not used to being outside, forcing it to be outside on its first night can also cause distress and in anything but warmer climates, it is potentially harmful as well. Try and find a compromise such as placing the pup's bedding in a laundry area that has outside access but also prevents the pup from feeling totally isolated from the family.

It is crucial that the pup is held in a secure area so that it cannot get out onto the street or come to harm in any other way, such as falling into a pool or gaining access to potentially aggressive dogs next door. Pups are small and flexible and have a knack of being able to get under gates and through gaps in fences.

## The First Days

Pups will often cry on their first night away from their mother and while this can make sleep for their new owners difficult, it usually doesn't last too long. After they have had their last feed they should go to sleep for

*Pups love to explore! Make sure they can't get into potentially harmful situations.*

the evening, though it is important to let the pup know that you are close at hand. You can check in on a regular basis and take them out for a toilet break but it is not good to come running at the first sound they utter. They will quickly learn that to get attention, all they need to do is start whining.

The activity level of puppies will vary greatly between different breeds and between individuals. One characteristic that is common to all puppies is the need for frequent sleeps. Families with children need to be aware that the pup needs to rest. When their activity level begins to slow, they should be allowed to go to sleep. They will usually want to sleep shortly after a meal. Putting them in the area where their bedding is located will help reinforce this as an area where they are safe, and should go to for sleep. They will begin to feel comfortable in this area and therefore they are less likely to whine at night.

It is also important to make children understand that pups can initially feel very insecure. Try to make the introductions to other family members a positive experience. Use lots of encouragement, stroking and gentle play. Avoid loud, harsh noises and rough handling. Pups shouldn't be encouraged to play in a manner that includes biting and growling by teasing and tormenting them. It might be fun when they are little but the novelty wears off as they get older and stronger and the pup will not understand why this type of play is no longer acceptable.

If you have other animals in your household you will need to be careful during the introduction process, particularly with older dogs. Being attacked by an older dog can leave a

*It is important to allow young pups and dogs to rest.*

Bringing Your Puppy Home

lasting impression on a puppy and adversely affect its socialisation with other dogs in the future. They can become very timid towards other dogs or alternatively become defensive and aggressive because they fear a repeat attack. Thankfully many older dogs are more sympathetic towards puppies than they may be to another adult dog. They seem to see them as less of a threat, but never underestimate the possibility of problems resulting from an interruption to the older dog's routine and territory.

All initial introductions should be done with the older animal leashed so that you have better control over the dog. It may also be beneficial to use an area away from the older dog's territory such as the front yard. If this is successful, the older dog can be released but you should stay with the dogs at all times to rescue the pup if play gets too rough. It is important to give your older dog plenty of attention during this time to prevent it from considering the puppy competition. If there is any suggestion that the older dog becoming too rough and the younger pup is showing fear, they should not be left alone together. However, you must allow the older dogs to establish their own relationship with the pup – just monitor their activities to ensure no one gets hurt!

*You need to monitor the activities of pups and older dogs to make sure that no one gets hurt!*

Puppies need to learn very quickly that other animal species in the house are not fair game! It is important when introducing them to household cats for example, that the cat is always able to stay out of reach of the pup if it chooses and vice versa. All interactions between puppies and other animals should be closely monitored. It is critical to train the puppy by setting limits with smaller species right from the start – it must learn quickly that it is not allowed to play biting games with the pet budgie!

As mentioned earlier, consistency is extremely important if your dog is expected to learn acceptable behaviour. This needs to begin as soon as you bring your puppy home. Puppies don't understand retrospective correction, which basically means that there is no point in getting angry with your puppy for something that it did earlier in the day, because it won't understand. You can only intervene at the time an undesirable behaviour is occurring. If you don't want them to do something, it is best to teach them what you would prefer them to do instead. If you can't be bothered, they will not understand why they can do something sometimes, and not others. For instance, if you don't want them to jump on the furniture you should never put them on the furniture and you should make the furniture inaccessible for them to reach on their own. Dogs enjoy routine so choose an area that is acceptable and comfortable for them lay down, like a mat or a dog bed

*You can't expect a puppy not to chew.*

which becomes their place. The puppy should be rewarded with praise and attention when it chooses its own bed. With time and through habit, the puppy will automatically choose the area it feels comfortable with instead of the furniture.

Chewing inappropriate items like shoes can also be a problem. You can't expect them not to exhibit normal puppy behaviour such as chewing, particularly when teething, but it is unreasonable to expect them to know that shoes are not toys. Inappropriate items such as shoes should be made inaccessible and toys, Nylabones™, sterilised natural bones and good quality rawhide chews can be provided to satisfy the need to chew and preserve your precious footwear. Rawhide chews can be problematic if the puppy eats them rather than chews them so you need to monitor their use. Old shoes should never be given because your pup is unlikely to be able to distinguish between these and your best shoes. There are other household hazards that are important to steer your puppy away from as soon as possible but these will be discussed a little later in this chapter.

## Diets and Feeding Regime

Most dogs are close to fully grown by the time they are twelve months of age. Such rapid development requires high levels of nutrition that are not provided by adult dog foods, table scraps, milk or raw meat. Feeding these types of foods, particularly table scraps and un-supplemented meat only diets can lead to severe bone growth disorders.

There are many different diets being used successfully by breeders around the world. Some use commercially prepared diets, others fresh food diets, and others may use a combination of both. If you feel confident in the breeder that you have chosen to buy your puppy from, you can be guided by them. Look closely at the quality of their breeding stock, and if they show their dogs, the consistency of their success in the showring. A poor diet will ruin the chances of success of even the most well bred animals.

For people with busy lifestyles, commercially prepared puppy foods that are formulated to meet the needs of growing pups, are probably the most convenient and the most commonly recommended by veterinarians. Although the labels on commercial puppy foods would appear to suggest that they are all equally beneficial, there are 'premium' foods and 'budget' foods. Some use lower quality ingredients that affect the digestibility of the product, resulting in more droppings and less growth. The price of a product is not always the best guide as many foods that are imported are more expensive, without necessarily being better.

Commercially prepared puppy foods are generally available in three forms. These are wet diets, which are your canned foods, moist diets that look like compressed meat in a plastic wrapper, and dry foods. Dry foods are most favoured by veterinarians for several reasons. Canned foods have a high water content which means that your dog receives far less nutrition per meal than it would for the equivalent volume of dry food. Semi moist diets contain less water than canned foods, but still have much higher water content than dry foods. The high water content makes these foods less 'value for money' but apart from the cost of feeding wet diets, dogs fed on these types of foods are more likely to develop problems with their teeth as they get older. The dry 'kibble' diets have an abrasive effect on the dog's teeth, helping to keep them clean. However, dry food diets can occasionally cause problems relating to particles becoming lodged in the gums causing infection and cavities so teeth and gums should be monitored regularly. Dogs on good quality dry diets are generally less likely to develop digestive problems and have less bulky droppings. In addition they are easy to store as they require no refrigeration.

*Commercially prepared puppy foods are available in moist diets (left) that look like compressed meats and wet diets (right) which are your canned foods.*

Some breeders warn against commercial diets because of the colours and preservatives that some contain. Although relatively uncommon, food allergies may result from these types of ingredients and some dogs can be intolerant of high carbohydrate, grain based diets. If you feel strongly about wanting to source an alternative diet to those commercially available, you should be guided by someone who is successfully using a fresh food diet. You could also check the diet and feeding regime that you have chosen with your vet. There are many diets that can be sourced on the internet that may sound good but they have had no clinical trials done to verify their effectiveness. Home cooked diets and raw food diets run a high risk of providing a serious imbalance of protein, fat, amino acids, vitamins and minerals if not done properly. Supplements are available that can be added to fresh food diets but unless you have some guidance or have the skills of a nutritionist, required to properly balance the diet for optimum growth, you run the risk of causing developmental growth problems. For instance the over supplementation of calcium can cause damage to bone development. Fresh food diets also require some dedication on the part of the owner, as they can also be more time consuming to prepare. They may also use bone from chicken carcasses as their main source of calcium. Just as some dogs may have difficulty digesting high carbohydrate diets, others may have some difficulty digesting diets with high bone content.

*Dry food diets are favoured by many veterinarians. They can have an abrasive effect on teeth keeping them clean.*

Feeding a premium puppy diet, fresh or commercial, will help avoid any muscle and bone development problems so it is worth trying to identify a diet that is considered to be 'premium' by both vets and breeders. In addition to identifying a good quality puppy diet, an experienced vet should be able to recommend a diet and feeding regime that is particularly suited to the type of puppy you have. They may also be able to recommend commercial puppy diets that do not contain artificial colours and flavours, while still providing good nutrition levels for your growing pup. If you choose the wrong diet for an adult dog you can generally change the diet and reverse the effect. However, the growth rate that your puppy experiences is so rapid that it is impossible to correct the damage that can be done after a short period of time on a poor or unbalanced diet.

I have already mentioned the need to avoid rapid changes in your puppy's diet that may cause a stomach upset. If you have decided to change the diet from the one the pup was on when you got it, make the

*Dogue de Bordeaux Puppies
Feeding a premium diet will help avoid muscle and bone development problems.*

changeover very gradual. Begin by introducing a small amount of the new food to each meal. Gradually increase the proportion each day until the new diet is being fed exclusively. The process should take a minimum of four days, preferably longer if there are any signs of diarrhoea. If the diarrhoea is severe, seek advice from your vet, as a change of diet is not the only cause. Dehydration due to ongoing diarrhoea is a serious problem in itself.

It can be difficult for small pups to handle dry food, particularly when they are teething and fussy pups may be less inclined to eat totally dry diets. In the beginning it may help to soften the dry food by soaking it, or by mixing a small amount of canned or semi-moist puppy food with the dry food. As they get older they will become accustomed to eating the dry food without adding water or other foods. Some people like to give puppies milk with their dry food. Milk contains the sugar lactose which dogs are unable to digest properly. They don't produce the correct digestive enzyme required to be able to digest the milk, frequently resulting in diarrhoea. If you insist on giving your pup milk, choose commercially available low lactose milk.

*Clean drinking water should be available at all times.*

Clean drinking water should be available at all times. Lack of water will kill an animal far more rapidly than lack of food. In addition to normal fluid requirements, dogs need extra water to re-hydrate the dry food in their stomach. The rapid growth rate of puppies also increases their need for water. Contaminated water can result in bacterial infections such as E.coli and parasitic infections such as Giardia and Cryptosporidium. Apart from making your dog ill, an affected dog can also pass the problem on to family members. It is in your best interest to keep your dog's water clean.

After weaning onto solid food, pups should receive at least three meals a day. Some may benefit from a fourth meal for a couple of weeks if they are younger than eight weeks old when you get them. It is preferable that this feeding regime should continue until they are six months old. As mentioned earlier, it is important for you to be there to feed, rather than leaving a bowl of food for the pup to eat when it pleases. The reason for this is that it helps to develop a routine which is beneficial for toilet training. Most pups will want to relieve themselves and sleep after a meal. If you know something is likely to happen, it is easier to set things up so that you can reward the pup for going to the toilet in the right place. By being there you can also make sure that your pup is getting the food that is provided. If you have other pets, they may consume food that is left out for your pup, or it may be eaten by other animals such as birds, cats and vermin. After six months of age you should be able to drop the midday feed and after twelve months, once or twice daily should suffice for most dogs. Twice is preferable for some breeds as it helps reduce hunger related behaviour problems and helps maintain blood sugar levels.

Most commercial dog foods provide a feeding guide somewhere on the packaging. While this can be helpful it is only a guide. The metabolism of puppies will vary from animal to animal, as do the activity levels and appetite. It is important not to allow greedy pups to become obese as this can lead to health issues later in life such as diabetes. Pups that are encouraged to eat more than they require in order to grow bigger or faster than their genetic background dictates, can end up with bone and joint abnormalities. Pups seem to grow up and out in spurts. It is not unusual for pups to go through a gangly, weedy stage. It is nothing to worry about as long as the pup is on a good diet, is being kept parasite free, and is maintaining reasonable body weight. If you have any concerns about the weight and development of your pup, it is best to consult your veterinarian.

*It is important not to allow greedy pups to become obese as this can lead to health issues later in life such as diabetes.*

Treats are an important part of training which should be started as soon as possible. Be aware that, if used in excess, they can affect the calorie intake of your pup and possibly reduce its appetite at meal times. Be careful not to overdo it during training sessions. Some food items that might be a treat for a human can be toxic to dogs. For instance chocolate, macadamia nuts and grapes can be toxic to dogs so you need to be particularly careful if children have access to these foods. Children may inadvertently give your puppy these types of treats without realising the consequences. Though less likely to be given as a treat, onions, if fed in reasonably large amounts can also cause haemolytic anaemia in dogs.

Bones can be considered both a treat food and an activity food. A large bone can keep a puppy occupied for a long time. For small pups however, it is best not to feed bones that are soft enough or small enough for the pup to be able to swallow. Small sharp bones, particularly chicken bones, can cause mouth trauma, get stuck in the pup's jaw or throat, or perforate the gut. Larger bone pieces can cause a bowel obstruction or

*Safer alternative to bones are good quality rawhide chews.*

obstipation (the inability to pass droppings). Large beef marrow bones however are ideal, as they will keep your puppy chewing but are too hard for a small pup to chew up and swallow. Small cooked bones are easily splintered and should not be fed. As pups get older bones can be added to the diet but they should always be fed in moderation. A safer alternative are good quality rawhide chews. These are completely digestible but will still be beneficial for the teeth, jaws and gums of growing puppies. There are differences in quality that relate to the manufacturing processes involved in their production. It is advisable to ask your vet to recommend a safe brand of rawhide chews that does not carry traces of potentially harmful chemicals.

## Toilet Training

One of the less pleasant aspects of owning a new puppy is cleaning up after all the little 'accidents' they tend to have when you first get them. The sooner they are toilet trained the better and there are different methods that can be used to achieve this end. Like most training exercises, it is best to set up the situation for success as this will lead to the most rapid result. To do this you need to look back at the wolf ancestry of your puppy again to make use of the natural instincts of dogs, in conjunction with some observation skills, and the implementation of a routine.

Anyone who has had a litter of puppies will know that good mothers will do their best to clean up any urine or faeces that their pups produce. This behaviour has nothing to do with our concept of cleanliness, remembering that dogs take great pleasure in rolling in smelly drains and dead animals! It is their instinctive need to protect their pups from predators by keeping the scent of their litter to a minimum. She will also do her best to make sure her own droppings are as far away from the litter as possible.

*Try to target a suitable toilet location and substrate as soon as you get home before your puppy forms a preference for somewhere less suitable.*

As pups get older they will often start to follow their mother's lead and move away from the sleeping area when they need to go to the toilet. Of course, pups are busy little creatures so sometimes they just forget, but the combination of instinct and learned behaviour from their mother is there, and is a basis to build on. When a pup is taken to a new environment it is important to try and target a new, safe and convenient toileting area for the pup. They will begin to form preferences for toilet location and substrate by seven or eight weeks of age so it's important to begin as soon as you bring your puppy home.

It helps to know that puppies will always need to relieve themselves when they wake up. If you see your pup beginning to wake up, you need to be ready to quickly escort it to the toileting area and praise the pup when it goes to the toilet. The area should be close enough to the house for the pup to reach easily. There is no point in targeting an area that is too far away, but try and choose an area that will be acceptable when they are older. Once they have adapted to the new area it is difficult to make them change again. It is also useful to use a verbal cue when the pup appears to be preparing to relieve itself. It doesn't really matter what word you use as long as the pup begins to associate the word with the action. The more often a pup is encouraged to use the same area for toileting, and is rewarded for successfully doing so, the more likely they are to attempt to go there automatically when they need to.

*It helps to know that puppies will always need to relieve themselves when they wake up so be ready to take your puppy to the toilet area.*

As mentioned in the previous section, establishing a routine will also help to set up situations where you can anticipate the likelihood of the pup needing to relieve itself. After meals is the best time to take the pup to the target area and use the word associated with going to the toilet when you see the preliminary behaviour begin. Going to the toilet is usually preceded by some ground sniffing, particularly as they get older. Some dogs seem to develop a ritual of behaviour before relieving themselves, such as needing to find tall grass, or weaving back and forth with their nose to the ground. Being observant of the pup's behaviour is the first step to stopping an accident before it happens. A puppy or dog that is confined inside the house cannot be expected to hold on when it needs to go to the toilet. Therefore there is no point in reprimanding a dog for having relieved himself when there was no other option. If you have successfully targeted an outside area, they will do their best to go to that area. If you can't leave the door open at all times so that the pup can achieve this goal, then taking the pup out regularly will help it to hang on. The routine will reassure the pup that an opportunity to go to the toilet will happen within a reasonable time.

If you catch the pup in the act of going to the toilet inside, when it has easy access to the outside target area, the most spontaneous reaction on the owner's behalf is usually to reprimand the pup. Unfortunately, this is interpreted by the pup as being a reprimand for relieving itself - a bodily function that cannot be avoided. They do not understand that the reprimand is associated with the place, not the action, as this type of thinking is too complex for a puppy. It is hard not to yell 'NO!' automatically but a better response would be to quickly interrupt the pup while it is in the act and transport it outside.

Crate training is another method that is commonly used and recommended by trainers and behaviourists. Crate training involves getting your puppy used to being confined to, and sleeping in, a transport crate. This is generally not difficult to do as dogs prefer to sleep in fairly small spaces. This relates to their ancestry where litters would have been protected from predators in a den. They find the security comforting and getting them used to the crate has the added benefit of making transport to a vet or other location in future less stressful. Following their mother's example, puppies do not want to soil the area where they sleep so they are more likely to hold on after eating or waking up if they are confined to the crate. After a meal your pup should be taken to the toilet area on a leash and given a minute or two to eliminate. If it chooses to run off and play instead, the puppy is taken back inside and confined to the crate for ten minutes. This is not intended as punishment. It is utilising the puppy's reluctance to soil the area where it sleeps to your advantage to set up a situation where you can be there to reward the puppy for using the toilet area. Your pup is then taken back to the toilet area and again given the chance to eliminate. The process is repeated until it eliminates in the targeted area after which it is praised and allowed to remain out and play. When your puppy cannot be directly supervised it can be confined to an exercise pen to keep it safe and to help facilitate toilet training. The crate can also be made available at all times for the puppy to retreat to as desired, and the crate the door can be closed at night for added safety.

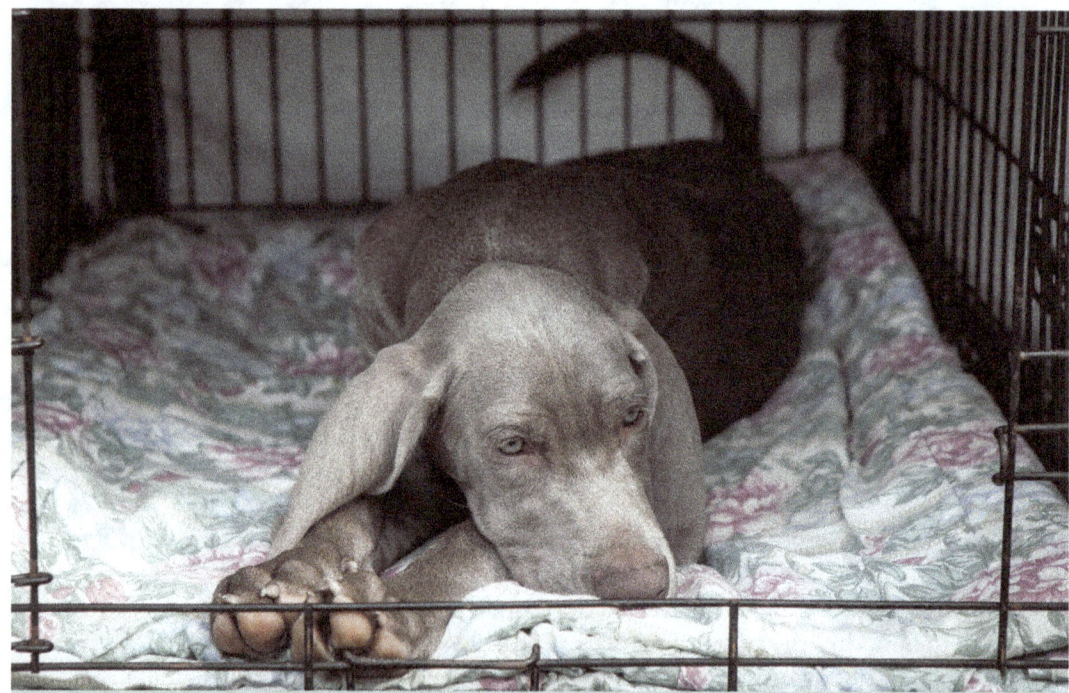

*It is usually not difficult to get puppies used to being in a crate as dogs prefer the security of retreating to a fairly small covered space to sleep.*

Another method that is commonly used is to target newspaper on the floor as the place that is acceptable for the puppy to go to when it needs to go to the toilet. If your pup needs to be confined to the inside of the house for long periods, this may be helpful. However, as pups form preferences for substrate very early, it may be beneficial to use a soil tray instead, to reinforce the preference for natural substrates for toileting. The idea is that the paper or soil tray is moved outside gradually, teaching the pup to go outside. Using this method makes cleaning up after the pup easier, but it teaches the pup that it is okay to go to the toilet inside, close to your sleeping area - as long as there is paper or a tray on the floor. In reality we would prefer that the dog use a toileting area as far away as possible and by reinforcing its instincts you are more likely to achieve this goal.

## Lead Training

Puppies should be trained to walk on a lead before taking them out in public. Some pups are not at all bothered by the sensation of being restrained around the neck. Others can be easily frightened, so it is essential that time is taken with these puppies to avoid making lead training a negative experience.

To begin with it helps to get nervous puppies used to having something around their neck. Attaching a fixed collar is the first step and most pups will quickly forget that the collar is there. Remember that puppies grow rapidly, so fixed collars should be checked and adjusted regularly before they have a chance to get too tight. When a lead is first attached, puppies that become alarmed by the sensation of the lead should be allowed to run around freely with the lead attached. This will help them get used to this object following them. They should never be left alone with the lead attached in case in gets caught on something. This would make the situation far worse as it would reinforce the fear of the lead, and could result in the puppy being physically harmed. The lead should be left on for 15 or 20 minutes during a play session. This can be repeated two or three times a day until the pup shows no fear of the lead being attached. You can make these sessions a positive experience by rewarding the pup with a treat as you attach the lead.

*You can make these sessions a positive experience by rewarding the pup with a treat as you attach the lead.*

The next step is to pick up the end of the lead and either call the pup towards you with gentle pressure on the end of the lead or try to get the pup moving towards a third person. A treat should be used to reward the forward motion either by yourself, if you encouraged the pup to come to you, or by the other person if the pup was encouraged to move towards them. It is essential that the puppy is not dragged along by the lead. Always encourage your puppy along with a happy, positive tone in your voice and frequent praise. Carrying treats with you is also a good idea to keep the pup focused on you rather than pulling away from you on the end of the lead. Your pup will quickly learn that the lead is a good thing, promising walks or treats!

## Keeping Your Puppy Safe

Many people are unaware of the potential hazards that a new pup may encounter. The first thing you need to be aware of is the threat of infectious disease. Puppies are generally sold after having had only one vaccination. The first vaccination may vary from country to country depending on what infectious diseases are common to the area where the pup was bred. Regardless of which diseases the vaccination protects against, the first vaccination provides only partial immunity, designed to bolster the pup's maternal immunity. Because of this, puppies should not be taken to public open places where unvaccinated dogs may have been until at least a week after

*It is important to keep lead training a happy and positive experience.*

their second vaccination at ten to twelve weeks of age. Puppies from disreputable puppy mills are often shipped when very young before even the first vaccination has had a chance to provide any protection at all.

It is crucial to socialise your puppy between eight and twelve weeks of age with both people and other dogs but you must be careful to avoid the risks associated with disease until the pup is fully vaccinated. The potential to come into contact with another infected puppy or a contaminated environment is quite high. Good breeders will already have started the socialisation process with other dogs that they own. You can continue the process by introducing them to other family members and friends but you may want to ask them to wash their hands and remove their shoes, particularly if they have dogs at home. You may consider visiting friends that have fully vaccinated dogs and as a general rule it is best to carry your puppy and avoid putting it down on potentially contaminated ground in public areas.

I have already mentioned the need to make sure that your yard is secure to prevent the puppy escaping into potentially hazardous environments. It is also important to check the yard itself for potential threats. These include making sure that your puppy can't drown in the backyard pool, or knock over large objects that it may crash into when playing. You should also make sure that there is no access to potentially toxic products that may be kept in the garden shed such as snail pellets, rodent bait, engine coolant, and fertiliser. The desire to chew and swallow inappropriate objects is also a concern. Electrical cords should be kept out of reach both inside and outside the house. Small objects and toys that are too small for the type of pup you have may be swallowed and result in a bowel obstruction or cause the puppy to choke. Make sure that the toys provided are robust enough to withstand chewing so that they don't break into pieces small enough to swallow.

Hazards associated with the environment such as poisonous snakes, spiders, paralysis ticks, and poisonous toads may vary according to where you live. Your vet or state kennel council can advise you on things that may pose a threat in your area. They are just like children in many ways and therefore a commonsense approach is required. You wouldn't leave a child in a hot car and the same applies to dogs. A couple of days of close observation will help you identify potential hazards. Rather than becoming alarmed or worried about your puppy's safety, simply be aware of what your pup is doing when it is awake and playing.

*Make sure that the toys provided are robust enough to withstand chewing so that they don't break into pieces small enough to swallow.*

*The desire to chew and swallow inappropriate objects is also a concern.*

*Rather than becoming alarmed or worried about your puppy's safety, simply be aware of what your pup is doing and enjoy their short lived puppyhood.*

# Getting an Adult Dog

*Weimaraner*

## Selecting an Adult Dog

The greatest advantage of taking on an adult dog is that there is no mystery about how the dog will develop physically and you can generally assess how friendly and outgoing the dog may be fairly quickly. Some people agree to re-home an adult dog that belonged to a friend or a relative and in this case, they will have some background information on the dog. However, if you have made a decision to take on an adult rescue dog you should be aware that these dogs often come without any pedigree, health or other background information. They may also have been abandoned or relinquished due to behavioural problems that may not be immediately obvious, especially if the dog appears friendly and outgoing. You will be providing a home for a dog with an unknown history, that may have had little or no training, and it is also possible that the dog may have been traumatised or abused by its previous owners. This type of dog may take some time to learn to trust you and transfer its loyalty to you as a new owner. They may also have some behavioural issues relating to their past treatment that will require the assistance of a trainer or behaviourist to help resolve.

If you have addressed these issues and believe you can meet a rescued dog's needs, contact a rescue organisation and discuss your situation with them. It can be extremely rewarding to be

*Rescued Salukis Amera and Bekki with their young companion Jazmyn.*

able to provide an abandoned and possibly abused animal, with a safe and loving home. However, in some cases it can be a long and difficult process and you may need more than the average level of dog handling skills, compassion, and commitment, to successfully integrate a rescue dog into your life and home. If you spend some time with a potential candidate at the shelter you may be able to determine the basic personality type of the dog and whether it has any obvious behavioural problems. Don't forget to ask if there is any history or background information available. Some rescue organisations use interim foster homes, so they may be able to give you some insight into the dog's behaviour and temperament. Some well loved pets have to be relinquished to a shelter or breed rescue centre because of family problems and these dogs often come with background information.

Many shelters will let you buy the dog and take it home on the understanding that if you are not compatible you can return the dog, so ask about this when you visit. Many of the points

*Rescue Greyhound 'Bella'*
*It can be very rewarding to offer a rescue dog a new and secure home.*

covered in Chapter 5 about selecting a healthy puppy will also apply to an adult dog such as examining the dog's eyes, ears, mouth, teeth and coat. While you are not selecting a show dog, being aware of potential health issues by looking closely at the dog will help you assess whether you are facing considerable veterinary expenses when taking on a rescue dog. You should be confident that you can meet these expenses before giving the dog a new home. Taking on an adult dog can avoid the difficulties of puppyhood, but it can also mean taking on any behavioural problems the dog may have developed from its previous situation. Many dogs end up in rescue because they were acquired as puppies but received no training from their owners. As they reach maturity they become unmanageable and are therefore surrendered to shelters. Many of these dogs will be fine with training but you need to be prepared to deal with them with understanding and patience. In some cases you may also need the help and guidance of a professional trainer or behaviourist, so you should factor this in as a possible expense as well.

## Meeting Other Family Members

If you already own another dog or other pets, it is important to consider how your decision to adopt a new dog will affect them. If your existing dog is aggressive towards other dogs, it is probably best not to attempt to bring another dog into the house, unless the new dog is a different sex and your dog's aggression is only directed towards dogs of the same sex. It would be unfair on the new dog to be confronted by another dog that was intent on inflicting harm. For the same reasons, dogs that have proved to be aggressive at the rescue shelter are best left at the shelter. It is hard enough to introduce an adult dog to your home without making it more difficult by making an unwise decision when selecting a dog. Many people make the mistake of thinking that only male dogs will fight but bitches can be as determined, if not more so, to seriously attack one another. A good shelter will be able to advise you on how tolerant one of their dogs is towards other shelter dogs. People with experience in training and dog behaviour may be able to work with dog aggressive animals, but tackling this problem for the less experienced is not a good idea unless you are prepared to seek professional help. These dogs are better suited to homes that do not have other animals to worry about.

*If you already own another dog or other pets it is important to consider how your decision to introduce another dog will affect them.*

Before your cat, bird or other small pets become 'dinner', it is best to assess the new dog's hunting or 'prey' drive. Don't be fooled into thinking that you can be watchful enough to prevent an unpleasant accident. Telephones ring, people knock on the door, and children can be forgetful. A dog intent on catching a 'prey' animal will always be ready to take advantage of any situation that distracts its owner - it only takes a few moments! You have a responsibility to protect your other animals.

*You need to assess you new dog's behaviour towards other pets.*

Bringing a new dog home is a strange experience for the dog. If the previous home was not a good one the dog may be nervous and insecure. It is important that everyone is positive and loving in their approaches so that it can feel reassured that the new home is a good place to be. It is important to watch interactions with children closely. If a dog has been abused, it may misunderstand the actions of children and respond instinctively to protect itself, resulting in harm to the children.

## Establishing a Routine

You need to take into account that your new dog has been displaced and may be very stressed in its new surroundings. It will take time to find its place in the family. As mentioned, you need to assess the dog's behaviour around children and small pets as these will be the most likely to be perceived as competition. Some dogs are naturally submissive and will happily become part of your family as long as there is plenty of attention and affection to go around. This is the ideal dog to introduce to your family. Other personality types can be fine; they just need to know where their place is in the family structure.

Consistency and routine are the keys to managing this situation. If the dog is to become part of the family, the human members of the family need to get together and establish consistent guidelines for dealing with the new dog. All members of the household must be consistent in their interactions with the new dog. Aggressive behaviour on the part of family members is not required in order to teach the dog how to behave in the home and this would only make an abused dog feel more insecure. Positive reinforcement training, a reward based method of training where good behaviours are rewarded and undesirable behaviour is ignored, is highly recommended. It is particularly beneficial in reinforcing suitable behaviour in the home and developing trust in dogs that may have been poorly treated in the past. Teaching behaviours using positive reinforcement methods such as clicker training has many benefits including being able to redirect the dog from undesirable behaviour by teaching the dog what to do instead. For instance, the new dog can be taught to sleep in its own bed by being rewarded when it chooses its bed, rather than the furniture to lie down in. More helpful information on positive reinforcement training can be found on our website at http://www.animalinfo.com.au.

*Dogs enjoy routine and knowing what belongs to them in terms of things like toys and bedding.*

Dogs enjoy routine. It gives them a sense of security knowing when they will be fed, when they will be let out to relieve themselves, and when they will go for a walk. Dogs like to know where they sleep, where they are allowed to go, and what belongs to them in terms of bedding, toys and food dishes. The sooner you establish a routine the sooner the dog will settle down and feel more relaxed. You must be aware that your routine may differ from what the dog was used to in its previous home so be patient and understanding. If you experience behaviours that you do not understand and are unsure of how to deal with, I suggest contacting a reputable dog behaviourist or trainer in your area. These trained professionals can often resolve an issue quickly and easily before it becomes a serious problem.

## Adopting an Older Dog

Apart from the issues already discussed, taking on an older dog may involve a few more things that you need to consider. They may take a little more time than a younger dog to adapt to new household rules, and therefore a little more patience may be required. On the other hand, they may have been taught perfect manners by their previous owners and have much less interest in being destructive.

*Older dogs may have been taught perfect manners by their previous owners and integrate easily into a new home, but others may feel less secure.*

Their health is one of the major concerns. You should be prepared to have a vet check them out to identify any health issues that require monitoring such as arthritis or diabetes. Older dogs require special diets designed to meet the geriatric body's needs - both in terms of minimising old age acquired weight, but also to meet changing nutritional needs. Obesity increases the likelihood of weight related illnesses such as heart disease and diabetes, and also aggravates arthritis and bone related disorders.

Older dogs may have spent all their life with one owner and may be very insecure in a new home. They will need a lot of attention and reassurance to make them feel at home. They are probably best suited to a home that does not have a lot of young boisterous children, but this may vary from one animal to the next, depending on the circumstances in their previous home. Many older dogs that are re-homed have been the companions of older people that have died. Therefore they may not be used to busy family homes with other animals and children. Children may inadvertently inflict pain on an arthritic dog so, if children are going to interact with an older dog, they must be taught to be gentle and read the warning signs that indicate when the dog needs to be left alone.

As long as you are sensitive to the needs of an older dog, giving a new home to an old soul can be very rewarding, even if it is only for a short time. However, it is important to realise that taking on an elderly dog can mean increased financial commitment. They may need more frequent vet trips and probably medication at some stage to improve the quality of their life.

*Rescue dog 'Teaser' taking a bow at the end of a 'Dancing with Dogs' performance. Older dogs from unknown backgrounds can be successfully trained.*

*Giving a secure new home to an older dog can be very rewarding.*

# Feeding Your Dog

## Introduction

After twelve months of age most dogs will suffice on one meal a day. However, there are occasions where maintaining more frequent feeds may be beneficial. For example, large and deep chested breeds such as Dobermanns, German Shepherds, Great Danes, and crosses of similar large breeds, may be prone to Gastric Dilation and Volvulus (Bloat). This extremely serious and potentially fatal condition requires urgent treatment if the dog is going to survive. It is thought that feeding smaller more frequent meals may help prevent this problem arising. Another reason for feeding more than one meal a day is that it helps maintain blood sugar levels and may help to keep your dog more relaxed and quiet, as a hungry dog may be more inclined to be noisy or destructive. However, over feeding dogs is also a major problem in domestic situations, so in many cases destructive and noisy behaviour is better prevented by providing activity toys rather than by feeding extra meals.

Choosing an unsuitable diet for an adult dog has less serious consequences than choosing an inadequate diet for a puppy. Because puppies grow so rapidly, feeding a poor diet can have an irreversible negative impact on their development. With adult dogs however, most negative impacts of an unsuitable diet can be reversed, if recognised early enough. It is advisable to always

*Border Collie from Working Lines*

*Large breeds such as Dobermanns may benefit from smaller more frequent meals.*

choose a good quality base product. However, to avoid boredom, to cater for fussy eaters, and dogs that may have food allergies, more variety and dietary options can be offered without too much risk.

## Commercial Diets

The principles of feeding commercial diets are basically the same for adults as those covered in the puppy section earlier in this book. There are high and medium quality commercial diets but also many others that are made with lower quality ingredients. The high quality diets usually have better digestibility and therefore better nutrient absorption and less waste production. This translates into better dog health and less droppings to clean up. There are also moist and semi-moist diets available for adults and these have higher water content than commercial dry foods.

*There are also moist and semi-moist diets available for adults. These have higher water content than dry foods.*

Identifying a good quality product may not be easy. Price is not always the best guide but your vet or a reputable breeder may help you decide on a good product. To complicate the issue, a premium product that comes highly recommended by vets and breeders, may be considered inedible by your dog. If your dog won't eat the product, or it has an adverse reaction to one of the ingredients, it is obviously not the diet for you. Moist diets are often more palatable so the combination of a top quality dry food and a moist diet stirred together may help to get your dog to accept the diet provided. Cooked and raw meats can also be added but you should be aware that many vets warn against the use of raw meat due to the potential for bacterial and parasitic infections. The main nutritional needs that your diet needs to meet are as follows:

## Protein

Being primarily carnivorous animals, protein in the form of quality meats or meat meals is the most important component of your dog's diet. Protein is expensive and your better quality products can be identified by the type of protein listed. Products that include specified fresh meat such as chicken or beef, and meat meals that are named, such as 'chicken meal' or 'beef meal', are generally better quality products. Meat meals are not considered an inferior source of protein. They are produced from cuts of meat that are not for human consumption but do not include hair, feathers, hoofs, and heads. They include the correct ratio of calcium/phosphorous and have lower water content than fresh meats. Products containing lower quality meat 'by-products' are best avoided, particularly if this is the main source of protein.

## Carbohydrates

Whole grains are the primary source of these nutrients. Dogs have difficulty digesting grains unless they are cooked or ground. Once processed (cooked), they are highly digestible and valuable in providing energy for your dog. Some dogs are sensitive to gluten so, for these dogs, it is better to choose low-gluten grain products such as those containing rice. Most dogs have no problems with high-gluten grains and better products are those containing whole grains rather than grain fragments and flours.

## Fibre

Processed diets have much higher carbohydrate content than natural wild carnivore diets. Fibre is found in vegetables and carbohydrates and although it cannot be digested by dogs, it is a necessary requirement to help their digestive system process high carbohydrate, low moisture dry food diets. Diets that use carbohydrates naturally high in fibre such as brown rice may not require additional fibre. Other diets may use isolated additional fibre sources such as beet pulp. Fibre in the form of hulls from grain and nuts is to be avoided.

## Fats and Oils

Obesity is one of the most common health issues in pet dogs today. However, fats and oils are a necessary part of your dog's diet, particularly beneficial for the skin and coat, but also required by other body processes and functions. Some products are high in saturated fat and lower in the more beneficial fatty acids. Try and identify products that have named fats and oils such as chicken fat and sunflower oil, and high levels of Omega 6 and Omega 3. The ratio of these two fatty acids needs to be 7:1 or less. Avoid products with non-specific ingredients such as animal fat and vegetable oil.

*Obesity is a common health issue in pet dogs.*

## Supplements

All commercial dog foods are required to contain vitamins and minerals to meet minimum nutritional standards. Some of the supplements may be destroyed during the manufacturing process but the better quality products have additional supplements added after the product has cooled. There are also better quality vitamins and minerals that are more easily absorbed. Chelates and sequestered minerals have far better absorption than sulphates and oxides such as zinc oxide. It is best to feed a high quality food that contains all of the ingredients needed by your dog, than to feed a poor quality diet with added supplements.

## Fruit and Vegetables, Flavours, and Sweeteners

Fruit and vegetables can provide vitamins and minerals but are generally only present in small amounts and are largely unnecessary in processed diets. They may provide additional fibre to diets using low quality carbohydrates but products with better quality protein, fats and carbohydrates are a better choice than products that contain lower quality ingredients with the addition of vegetables. Onions, grapes and raisins should never be given as these can be toxic to dogs. Flavours, colours and sweeteners are also unnecessary and included primarily for marketability purposes. Sweeteners and flavours are often added to poor quality diets to improve palatability. While some flavours such as beef stocks and broths are not harmful, sweeteners can add to the risk of diabetes and other health issues. In addition, sweeteners can be addictive, making it difficult to switch dogs to a higher quality product that does not use sweeteners. Chocolate is also toxic and should never be given to your dog.

### Preservatives

It is difficult to entirely eliminate preservatives from your dog's diet. Even if they have not been added to the final product, they may already be present in some of the ingredients. Good quality ingredients require fewer preservatives and some products use natural preservatives such as vitamin E, and various herb extracts. Products with high levels of chemical preservatives are best avoided.

*Assuming that you eat a reasonably healthy diet, adding table scraps to your dog's food may not be a bad thing.*

Assuming that you eat a reasonably healthy diet, adding table scraps to your dog's food may not necessarily be a bad thing, although to avoid an annoying begging habit, it is best to put the food into your dog's bowl rather than to give it directly from the table. Scraps to avoid using are those that are high in sodium and fat. Adding the fat trimmed from raw meat cuts may also lead to an obese dog. The more things you add to your dog's diets the more careful you need to be in your choice of commercial diet. A good quality commercial diet will help offset the negative impact of anything that you add that may imbalance the diet. It is always a good idea to ask your vet about the diet you are feeding. They will generally be happy to give you an opinion on the foods and feeding regime you are using.

More details and advice on the dietary requirements of dogs, common myths associated with feeding dogs, and selecting from the myriad of commercial diets on the market, can be found at the 'The Dog Food Project' - http://www.dogfoodproject.com .

### Fresh Foods

Many vets will recommend feeding a commercial diet to their clients. As many dog owners don't have the time to spend preparing a balanced fresh food diet, vets see these products as a simple way of providing a good diet for their clients' dogs. Critics of commercial diets suggest that the primary reason for this recommendation is because vets sell these products and earn revenue from their sale. These critics, including some vets and reputable breeders, may recommend a more traditional carnivore diet, based on replicating the feeding habits of wild dogs. This type of diet is generally referred to as a "Bones and Raw Food" diet (B.A.R.F.).

Advocates of raw food diets claim that many poor health issues in domestic dogs can be traced back to the use of grain in commercial diets, as well problems arising from sensitivity to artificial colours, preservatives and flavours used in the production of some of these products. There is no doubt that there are dogs that have allergies to some of these products and dietary alternatives must be found for these dogs. On the other hand, many vets suggest that the bones and raw food diets pose a far greater threat to the health of dogs. Problems that are suggested to arise from this type of diet are heart and kidney problems, brain illnesses, parasitic and bacterial infection and severe life threatening pancreatitis. Vets warn that sudden death can occur in dogs fed on bones and raw food diets, resulting from continuous damage to the stomach and intestines by the fine bones of chicken and turkey necks that form a large component of many of these diets.

One important thing to remember is that a wild dog or wolf hunting live prey would eat the entire animal. Raw meat alone, without bones, organs, stomach and digestive tract contents, cannot be compared to wild diets and will lead to dietary deficiencies. There is also the assumption that wolves are automatically healthy as a result of their wild diet, however, wild dogs and wolves that have been brought into captivity are often malnourished. Studies done on carcasses have also shown that wolves have died of bowel perforations caused by fowl bones and frequently have serious dental problems. Supplementation of bones and raw food diets is highly recommended to help ensure a balanced diet. Fresh food diets containing cooked meat, grains, and vegetables enjoy far greater acceptance by vets. Cooking helps eliminate parasites and bacteria that may cause illness in your dog and helps the dog digest and utilise the nutrients in grain and fresh vegetables.

*Wolf with Caribou Hindquarter*
*One thing to remember is that a wild dog or wolf hunting live prey would eat the entire animal.*
*Photo - Denali National Park and Preserve*

There are some excellent dietary alternatives to feeding a dry food diet. The only requirement is some solid research into the diet, the time needed to prepare the diet, and preferably some consultation with your vet on the pros and cons of the diet you are proposing to use. A feeding trial is also recommended but you need to allow at least six weeks, preferably more, to adequately assess the effects of the diet. Unfortunately, some serious consequences of nutritional deficiencies can take much longer to become apparent. There can also be serious consequences resulting from the excessive intake of some nutrients, hence the importance of consulting with your vet before making any radical dietary decisions.

Whether or not you feed primarily dry food, cooked food, raw food, or a combination of both, bones in moderation are a welcome addition to your dog's diet. Although dry diets are considered to have an abrasive effect on teeth, helping to prevent tartar build up, gingivitis, and periodontal disease, a good bone to chew on will always be enjoyed and also help to exercise the gums and remove tartar. Feed raw bones only, as cooked ones may splinter causing damage ranging from minor cuts to the gums and mouth, to perforated intestines, as mentioned earlier, causing death. Chicken necks and wings are good for smaller dogs, ranging through ribs, neck bones, shanks and long leg bones from sheep and cows for the bigger dogs. Feeding large marrow bones can be beneficial, as many dogs

*Bones in moderation are a welcome addition to your dog's diet, helping to exercise gums and remove tartar.*

do not have the strength to break the bone into small pieces. However, some dogs will continue to grind away at bones, ingesting small amounts that can still cause digestive problems, while some large dogs can break and swallow large pieces.

As mentioned earlier with regard to the B.A.R.F. diet, a potential health issue associated with too much bone in the diet is obstipation/intractable constipation. This painful condition may require a general anaesthetic to remove impacted bone from the rectum and intestines. Too much marrow can also predispose your dog to pancreatitis or trigger an attack if your dog already suffers from this condition. Broken teeth can result from chewing on bones as well as

*Offering rawhide chews may be a safer alternative to raw bones.*

fragments becoming lodged in the upper palate and between the teeth. You should monitor your dog carefully to see how well it digests and eliminates bones before offering bones on a regular basis. Offering rawhide chews and only the occasional bone may be a safer alternative.

## Special Needs

### Older Dogs

The life span of dogs varies between breeds quite dramatically. Determining the age at which dogs are considered older is therefore relevant to the breed, but also to the health and activity level of individual animals. Crossbred dogs can be more difficult to assess due to the obscurity of the breeds in their genetic background. As a general rule larger dogs have shorter life spans and dogs that are in the latter third of their life, relative to their estimated life span, are considered 'older'. As it can be difficult to judge the age of your dog if it is active and healthy, their diet may not need to be changed just because you think they may be technically 'older'. Dietary changes are meant to compensate for age related changes in your dog. If these changes are not apparent due to the fact that your dog is healthy and active you may not need to worry too much about changing their diet. However, making dietary changes that improve the absorption of nutrients may also help to prolong your dog's life by delaying age related changes. Asking your vet's opinion on when your dog should be considered a 'senior' at your dog's yearly health check will help you determine when to alter its diet.

*Making dietary changes that improve the absorption of nutrients may also help to prolong your dog's life.*

Older dogs tend to become overweight through lack of exercise and overfeeding, or underweight, possibly as a result of deteriorating dental health or other health issues. For overweight older dogs a diet that is lower in fat (10%-12%), and therefore lower in calories is recommended, as well as reducing the amount of food given if necessary. Dogs that are losing weight as they get older should be thoroughly checked by a vet who can try and determine the reasons for the weight loss. Food may need to be moistened and warmed or otherwise softened if they are having difficulty chewing. Feeding smaller meals more often may encourage them to eat more.

As renal failure can be a common problem in older dogs, lower protein also puts less pressure on kidneys. A diet of 18% protein is generally recommended for healthy dogs, while those that have been diagnosed with kidney failure are generally placed on diets as low as 14% protein. Older dogs have difficulty absorbing nutrients from the digestive tract and lose more through the urinary tract. Supplements can be added to help combat this loss and balance the diet. Older animals also tend to suffer from constipation and therefore diets with higher fibre content (3%-5%) are more suitable. The addition of wheat bran to fresh food diets or standard dry food diets can help to raise the fibre content.

There are commercially prepared diets for older dogs and as with standard diets, there are good products and others that are poorer quality. They also

*It is best to discuss the supplementation of your older dog's diet with your vet to make sure that the supplements provided are suitable.*

tend to be more expensive, so your vet may be able to recommend minor changes to your standard diet, without the added expense of purchasing a special diet. Some supplements can help to combat age related health issues such as joint disease and arthritis. For instance, Glucosamine and Chondroitin added to the diet may help to improve joint mobility. Antioxidants are also thought to slow the aging process. Fatty acids can improve the condition of the coat and skin, particularly in older dogs. It is best to discuss the supplementation of your older dog's diet with your vet to make sure that the supplements and quantity provided are suitable for your dog.

## Overweight Dogs

The activity level of dogs varies between breeds and between individual animals, regardless of breed. Generally however, dogs are keen to play games and go for a walk. The idea of a dog being 'fat and lazy' has more to do with the 'fat' part than being lazy by nature.

Overweight dogs often become lethargic, a condition that accelerates the weight gain and leads to other health issues such as joint disease. There is also the greatly increased risk of heart disease and diabetes to consider.

Allowing a dog to become fat is easily done. Some dogs are also more inclined to store fat and become overweight, even if the meals given are the recommended amount for the dog's size and age. The dogs that are inclined to put on weight are often masters of the 'I am a poor starving animal look' that is hard to resist. Those pleading eyes will often net them a haul of titbits that far exceeds their daily dietary needs. Food motivated dogs will raid bins, steal from the table, and snatch or beg for food from children. To control weight gain in this type of dog it is extremely important to be aware of how much food the dog is soliciting from other sources during the day.

Getting your dog to lose weight may be a simple as removing the snacks or stolen food from the daily diet. If this is too difficult the daily meal should be adjusted to compensate for the snacks. There are low fat 'light' commercial diets that can be used. Rather than giving a small meal, some of the daily meal can be replaced with cooked vegetables that will not add weight, but will help to give the dog a feeling of fullness.

Reducing a dog's daily fat and calorie intake is only part of the solution. To lose weight effectively and help the dog regain normal activity levels, exercise is needed. Over-exercising an overweight animal that has become unfit can be dangerous to their heart, so a steadily increasing exercise program is required in conjunction with dietary changes. A regular walk is a good place to start and exercise levels can be increased as the dog loses more weight. At a certain point, the lethargy will begin to lift and the dog will be much more inclined to want to exercise and move around. The more it exercises, the more rapid the weight loss. A dog may be able to return to a normal calorie and fat intake diet, once the weight has been lost and normal activity levels have resumed.

Under no circumstances should an overweight dog be placed on a starvation diet that does not meet the dog's daily nutritional requirements both in volume and nutrients. The diet still needs to be balanced and there are serious health threats resulting from sudden weight loss which can affect the liver, and be potentially

*Pleading eyes will often net dogs titbits that far exceed their daily dietary needs.*

life threatening. Your vet can help you develop a diet, feeding, and exercise regime that will help your dog regain normal weight and activity levels. Just bear in mind that allowing your dog to become obese is a far greater form of abuse than letting it go without that titbit from the table!

*Black Pekingese*
*Regardless of breed, to lose weight effectively and help the dog regain normal activity levels, exercise is needed.*

## Food allergies and Special Diets

Food allergies can develop over a long period of time, so your dog may begin to show symptoms years after being stable on the same diet! It can show as itchiness, licking, rubbing, ear infections, flatulence and more rarely vomiting, diarrhoea and sneezing. If your dog is already on a premium food the chances of developing a food allergy will be lessened, but dogs can be allergic to one simple ingredient and it is often a long and painful process to eliminate all of the possible culprits. This is something you should seek your vet's advice on. There are special allergy diets available now that can be used short or long term while you gradually reintroduce other ingredients back into your dog's diet.

There are also special diets available for a variety of health related issues such as kidney, liver, and joint disease. These tend to be manufactured by companies that produce good quality diets and are based on sound research into common health issues, such as kidney failure in older dogs. Most are available from veterinary practices only and should be used on the recommendation of your vet.

*A good diet that is appropriate for the size, age, and type of dog is reflected in the dog's coat and overall condition.*

*Ten year old Nova Scotia Duck Tolling Retriever 'Alex'. Dogs enjoy playing as long as they remain fit and healthy and diet plays an important role.*

# Keeping Your Dog Healthy

## Visual Examination

Ownership of any animal includes being responsible for maintaining their health and wellbeing. Unlike children, they are unable to tell you when they are feeling unwell or when they are experiencing pain. It is up to you, the owner, to recognise signs and symptoms that may indicate a problem. One of the most important ways of doing this is through the use of simple observation skills. Being aware of what is 'normal' for your dog will help you identify any condition that is not.

If you have recently acquired your dog or puppy and you are unsure of its health status, it is best to take it to the vet for a check-up. Your vet can usually identify any general health issues that may be a problem and can also give you a few pointers on recognising poor health, such as coat and skin condition, body weight, teeth, and nails. Your dog will be weighed each time it visits the same vet so that they have a record of the dog's weight. If your dog receives a clean bill of health from the vet you will have something to identify as 'normal' for your dog. After that it is up to you to identify any variations that may indicate a problem.

You should familiarise yourself with the dog's gait and its general disposition when moving around and playing. Dogs that become inactive or snappy around children and other animals

*Dobermann*

*Familiarise yourself with what is 'normal' for your dog when it is in good health.*

may have an injury or be developing arthritis, or some other bone related disorder such as hip dysplasia. Swelling may result from an insect, reptile or animal bite, but may also result from broken bones or fractures that require x-ray. Inactivity may also indicate that the dog is getting too heavy and therefore lethargic. In the early stages, it is easy not to notice gradual weight gain or weight loss in a dog. Lethargy can also be an early warning sign of much more serious health issues. Heavy breathing and coughing after limited exercise can be symptomatic of a serious condition such as heartworm infestation or cardiac disease.

Changes in the clarity of eyes can indicate the onset of eye disease or an eye injury. Eyes and ears should be clear of discharge and the ears should not have a bad odour. Head shaking may indicate an ear infection, or a foreign body such as a grass seed. Most dogs moult twice a year, usually in conjunction with major seasonal changes (spring and autumn). The coat can be dull at this time but at any other times it should be in good condition. The dog's coat is one of the best overall indicators of good health. Poor diet, internal and external parasites, and many other health issues can be reflected in the condition of the dog's coat.

*Eyes and ears should be clear of discharge and ears should not have a bad odour.*

You should also familiarise yourself with what normal droppings and urine output are for your dog. Gradual changes may indicate a developing problem such as worm infestation or kidney problems. Excessive drinking, and the resulting excessive urine output, known as polydipsia and polyuria, is a classic indicator for some serious dog diseases. Any sudden changes to your dog's behaviour requires immediate attention. Serious diarrhoea, vomiting, convulsions, disorientation, stomach distension, weakness and bleeding all mean an emergency visit to the vet. Many dogs have a high tolerance to pain, and so by the time you notice they are in discomfort, a condition may have become quite advanced. Quick action on your part can mean the difference between life and death.

## Vaccinations

Vaccination protocols vary from country to country and will depend on what infectious diseases are prevalent in your area, how often your dog comes in contact with other dogs, and your dog's age and health. As a result of the development and implementation of vaccination programs, many of the diseases that vaccinations protect against are now relatively uncommon. However, they still pose a problem for kennels, rescue shelters and pet shops. Puppies that result from the uncontrolled breeding of unvaccinated parents often find their way to rescue shelters and pet shops. Kennels that show their dogs, or are involved with other dog related activities, are always in danger of bringing a disease home to their very young pups that are yet to begin their vaccination program.

After birth, the milk produced by the mother for the first 48 hours is known as colostrum, which contains antibodies that will help protect the pups from infection. Assuming the mother is fully vaccinated, pups are protected by these antibodies in their mother's milk until they reach six weeks of age, though the level of antibody protection can vary from pup to pup. A small pup may not have received as much milk in the first 48 hours as a stronger pup. The point at which the mother's antibodies begin to wane is the time that pups are most vulnerable. Kennels may need to use some quarantine protocols to prevent bringing disease home to their very young pups at this age. Pups cannot be vaccinated earlier than 6 weeks of age as the maternal antibodies are likely to recognise the vaccine as a potential infection, and block the effect of the vaccine. Most puppy vaccination programmes will involve the first vaccination at 6-9 weeks, the second at 12 weeks and then a third at 16 weeks, though the requirement for a third vaccination will vary from country to country. It can also depend on the type of vaccine used and what diseases are being vaccinated against.

*The milk produced by the mother for the first 48 hours is known as colostrum, which contains antibodies that will help protect the pups from infection.*

Standard or 'core' vaccines are those used against very serious infectious canine diseases that can be fatal, if contracted. There are also optional or 'non-core' vaccines that your vet may recommend if your dog is at risk of exposure to some of the diseases covered by non-core vaccines. Dog vaccines protect the animal in just the same way as vaccines for cats or humans. They work by exposing your dog to a small amount of a non-harmful form of a disease in order to stimulate your dog's immune system to develop antibodies to that disease. A vaccinated dog that is exposed to a harmful disease will be able to fight off the disease using its own immune system that has been stimulated by the vaccine.

The main core and non-core vaccinations are listed below:

### Core
- **CDV** - Canine Distemper Virus
- **CPV-2** - Canine Parvovirus 2
- **CAV-2** - Canine Adenovirus 2 - protects against Infectious Hepatitis
- **RV** - Rabies (required in all but rabies free countries)

### Non-Core
- **Bordetella** (Kennel Cough) - Recommended for dogs that have a lot of exposure to other dogs or that will be entering a boarding kennel.
- **Parainfluenza** - Another respiratory disease that can lead to pneumonia.
- **Lyme Disease** - Recommended for areas where Lyme disease carrying ticks are prevalent.
- **Leptospirosis** - Zoonotic (a disease that can be passed to humans). Vaccination can cause anaphylaxis (severe allergic reaction) in some breeds.

There are other non-core vaccines that are less likely to be recommended as they are specific to less common regional or environmental risks. Some non-core vaccines are included in polyvalent core vaccines. These are vaccines that are designed to protect against a number of infectious diseases or more than one strain or species of micro-organism (polyvalent). You may be offered a choice of vaccinations by your vet that will have different combinations of core and non-core vaccines. It is best to discuss the risks your dog may be exposed to with your vet before deciding on the best vaccination for your dog.

Vaccination is a crucial part of responsible pet ownership. The frequency of booster shots may vary depending on the recommendations of your vet, on the type of vaccine used, and sometimes on the law. In states in the USA where rabies is prevalent, all dogs must be vaccinated against rabies on a yearly basis by law, whereas every third year is all that is required in other states, where incidence of the disease is lower. In countries that are currently rabies free there is no requirement at all for vaccination. There is a growing trend amongst the veterinary community to reduce the frequency of vaccinations. Testing of the antibody levels or 'titres', has suggested that the protection received from vaccinations may last longer than previously thought. Deciding to vaccinate your dog less frequently should not be done without discussion with your vet, as it may not be worth the risk to your dog. It is best to tailor vaccination programs to the individual dog based on an assessment of the risk that the dog is exposed to. A yearly visit to the vet clinic will help your vet determine this risk and also allow them to perform a general check of your dog's health. Sometimes a booster will be recommended earlier than usual if your dog is about to enter a boarding kennel.

Some dogs may experience adverse reactions to some vaccines so a vet may recommend less frequent vaccinations for these dogs. This has been known to occur most frequently with some Toy breeds. Dobermanns and Rottweilers can be more prone to infection with parvovirus so your vet may recommend more frequent vaccinations against this disease in these breeds. Vaccinations are likely to be less effective in immune suppressed animals and live vaccinations should never be given to pregnant or lactating bitches. There are 'killed' or 'attenuated' vaccines that can be safely given. Always discuss the condition of your bitch with your veterinarian before vaccination. Dogs that have an unknown vaccination history such as those that find their way to rescue shelters should be checked by a vet, who will recommend an appropriate vaccination regime for the dog, based on their age and condition.

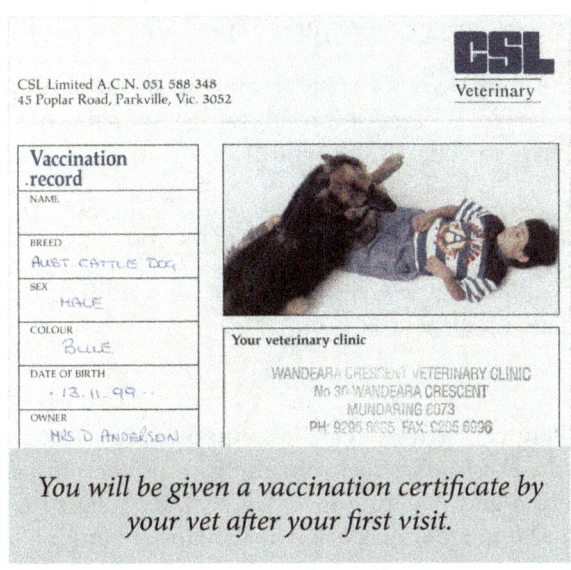

*You will be given a vaccination certificate by your vet after your first visit.*

You will be given a vaccination certificate by your vet after your first visit. This will need to be taken and updated at all repeat visits for boosters and may be required by kennels and training organisations before your dog is allowed to enter the facility.

Diseases that are prevented by core vaccines are potentially fatal and dogs should be taken to a vet as soon as symptoms become obvious. Other diseases that are prevented by non-core vaccines are less likely to be fatal, but your dog may suffer prolonged symptoms, and sustain some permanent organ damage, if these are not treated as soon as possible. Below is a brief description of the symptoms associated with each disease to help you recognise the onset of disease.

## Canine Distemper Virus (CDV)

Highly infectious. This disease is relatively unstable in the environment. As a result, transmission generally requires close animal contact, generally in the form of one dog inhaling virus particles from the coughing and sneezing discharge of another infected dog. Virus is also passed in other body secretions including urine and faeces, though contact with infected faeces carries lower risk unless the dropping was passed within 30 minutes.

Symptoms may begin with eye and nasal discharge. As the disease progresses symptoms include loss of appetite, high fever, vomiting, diarrhoea, coughing associated with the development of pneumonia and calluses of the nose and foot pads. Neurological symptoms develop in the latter stages of the disease and often begin with snapping and tremors of the jaw but may include general tremors, imbalance, and weakness of limbs.

## Rabies

This disease is not a problem in Australia, New Zealand and the United Kingdom which are rabies free. However it is a major problem in many parts of the United States. It is a zoonosis (a disease that can be passed to humans) and can also be transmitted between animals.

Transmission is usually via a bite from an infected animal. The disease can be carried by wildlife as well as dogs. Unfortunately symptoms may not be apparent until the virus reaches the brain 20-30 days after the animal, or person, was bitten. By this time there is no cure for animals or humans. When symptoms of the disease become evident, the dog begins shedding the virus and is then capable of transmitting the disease to people or other dogs and animals. The stages of the disease after symptoms appear are as follows:

**Prodromal Stage:** First 1 ½ days. Temperament changes become apparent and friendly dogs may appear shy. A change in voice may become apparent due to spasms in the larynx.

**Excitative Stage:** In the following 2 days the animal loses all fear and begins to suffer from hallucinations and becomes aggressive. The larynx is paralysed resulting in the inability to swallow. As a result the dog drools and appears to 'foam at the mouth'.

**Paralytic Stage:** In the following 2 days, weakness and paralysis become apparent. The animal dies as a result of paralysis of the intercostal muscles that control breathing.

Anyone that is bitten by a dog with an unknown vaccination history (or wildlife) in a country that has rabies should seek immediate medical attention.

## Bordetella

Highly infectious. Commonly known as 'kennel cough' as it can be common in commercial kennel complexes where it can spread rapidly. The Bordetella bronchiseptica bacteria infect the bronchi and trachea causing inflammation and resulting in a dry hacking cough that is similar to 'whooping cough' in humans. The incubation period is variable – between 2 and 14 days. Most healthy dogs will recover without treatment provided that the infection does not occur in conjunction with one of the more serious diseases such as distemper or parvovirus, resulting in pneumonia. Treatment may speed up recovery and involves antibiotics to kill the Bordetella organism and a cough suppressant to provide relief during recovery which can take several weeks.

## Canine Parvovirus

Highly infectious. This virus has been virulent for the past twenty years and is shed in large numbers by infected animals. As a result, environmental contamination is extensive. Only a small amount of virus is required to cause infection and can come from a puppy eating food from a contaminated environment or by licking itself after sitting on contaminated ground. Although it affects dogs of all ages, it is most severe in puppies. The prevalence of the virus in the environment is the reason that puppy owners are advised not to visit public areas frequented by lots of dogs. The severity of infection is relative to the immune status of the puppy and the number of virus particles that the pup is exposed to. Symptoms include vomiting, diarrhoea, excessive thirst, weight loss, listlessness, and appetite loss. Canine coronavirus produces the same symptoms but is less severe unless infection occurs simultaneously with parvovirus. In this instance the symptoms become more severe. As a result coronavirus vaccine, normally considered a non-core low priority vaccine, may be included in some combination vaccines.

## Infectious Hepatitis

Transmission is via the nose or mouth from contact with the faeces, urine, blood, saliva, and nasal discharge of infected dogs. The disease is caused by the Canine Adenovirus Type 1 and results in an acute liver infection. The virus replicates in the tonsils and passes to the liver and kidneys within four to seven days. Symptoms include fever, depression, loss of appetite, jaundice, coughing and a tender abdomen. Sometimes confused with parvovirus because the disease can also include a low white blood cell count and bloody diarrhoea. However there are other symptoms of liver disease that may become apparent such as vomiting, corneal oedema, haematomas (blood-filled swellings) in the mouth and hepatic encephalopathy (impaired brain function). Death can result from the disease but many dogs recover after treatment for the symptoms.

## Parainfluenza and Adenovirus Type 2

Highly infectious respiratory diseases that have similar symptoms to Bordetella but can lead to pneumonia and death in young pups. Often included in combination vaccines and recommended for dogs that will have contact with other dogs on a regular basis.

## Lyme Disease

This disease is transmitted by the bite of the Ixodes ticks carrying the bacteria Borrelia burgdorferi. Symptoms can include the sudden onset of severe pain and lameness, fever, loss of appetite and depression. The disease can lead to crippling joint, cardiac, kidney and neurologic disease. The ticks are widely distributed in the United States, United Kingdom and Europe and are carried by field mice, voles, sheep and horses. Vaccination is only recommended in areas where ticks known to carry the disease are prevalent.

*Ixodes ticks carry the bacteria Borrelia burgdorferi which causes Lyme Disease.*

## Leptospirosis

Zoonotic (can be transmitted to humans). It is also transmitted between animals. Rats are considered to be responsible for about one third of all infections in humans. Transmission is via urine from an infected host coming into contact with abraded skin (open wounds). General symptoms include fever, excessive thirst, joint pain, jaundice, nausea, depression and loss of appetite. Excessive bleeding can also occur due to low platelet levels. The disease can result in serious kidney and liver damage and can be fatal. The vaccination can result in anaphylactic shock in some animals, and has a lower successful protection rate than other vaccines. In light of this, vaccination should be given at the recommendation of your vet, relative to the risks posed to your dog.

## Endoparasites & Ectoparasites

New medications are continually being developed that aid in the control and treatment of internal (endo) and external (ecto) parasites. Heartworm and intestinal worms are the main internal parasites that will affect your dog, while fleas, ticks and mites are the most common external parasites. Medications are often combined in a single product that protects against a number of different parasites making the job of keeping your animal parasite free easier. The following are descriptions of the main parasites and their effects on your dog's health.

## Heartworm

Heartworm differs from intestinal worms in that transmission is via a mosquito bite, infection involves primarily the heart, lungs and blood vessels, and any dog can become infected, regardless of how clean you keep the dog's environment and how isolated it is from other dogs.

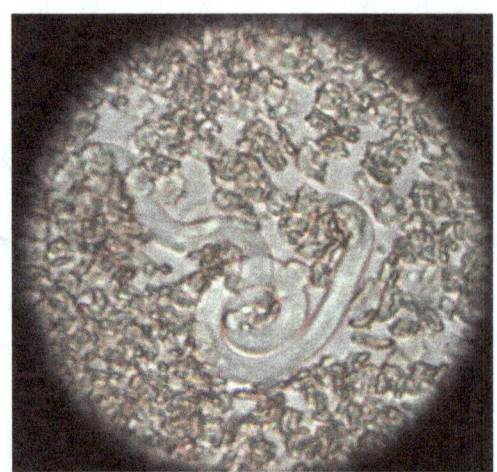

*Heartworm Microfilariae
Photo - Dr Joel Mills*

There is no environmental stage in the life cycle of heartworm but there are areas, particularly some regions in the United States, where infection rates in dogs that are not on preventative treatment, is as high as 45%. This is a direct result of mosquitos, carrying infective larvae, transmitting the infection from one animal to the next. Once infected, the larvae grow and develop in the new host until the worms become sexually mature and begin to reproduce approximately six months after infecting the animal. The tiny larvae known as microfilariae are released into the bloodstream where they grow and develop. Heartworm will take up to 12 months to fully mature, with females reaching 25 to 30 centimetres long (10 to 12 inches). Male worms are less than half the size and occasionally dogs can be infected with a single sex only which greatly reduces the clinical impact of infection. The worms are long lived, up to seven years, so even small numbers can eventually cause damage to vital organs. Less active dogs infected with low numbers of worms may never develop clinical signs of infection.

The organs most commonly affected are the heart and lungs. There may be no early signs of infection but usually the first symptom to appear as the disease develops is a cough, followed by exercise intolerance and some abnormal lung sounds. Severe disease is characterised by the same symptoms but the cough may become more pronounced, the dog will appear weaker and there may be loss of consciousness due to the lack of blood reaching the brain. The presence of abdominal fluid, an enlarged liver and abnormal heart sounds can all precede death.

There are several different ways of diagnosing heartworm infection. One of the most common is a blood sample, looking for the presence of microfilariae. Their presence in the bloodstream is considered definitive proof of infection but a negative test result may not rule out infection. Your vet will advise you on the most effective tests based on the condition of the dog, but tests may include x-rays and ultrasound to examine the extent of damage to the heart and lungs. Treatment for heartworm usually involves the administration of an adulticide to kill the adult worms. A different drug is used to eliminate the microfilariae.

*A German Shepherd Dog heart infected with heartworm. Photo – Dr Joel Mills*

Complications may arise from treatment as a result of large numbers of dead adult worms and lesions blocking the blood vessels. In most cases treatment is successful but prevention is better to avoid treatment complications and permanent organ damage. Heartworm preventative treatment must be started before a puppy is old enough to have developed heartworm disease. You should discuss preventative programs with your vet when your pup gets its vaccinations. An older dog might require testing to eliminate the possibility of infection before being started on certain preventative drugs. You should discuss the various treatment options and tests with your vet as there are several alternatives.

Many monthly preventative programs for intestinal worms and external parasites now include heartworm prevention. There are also daily pills and injections that can be administered yearly or twice yearly to prevent heartworm infection. If you choose either of these options, you need to be careful when selecting your worming and parasite treatments, or preventatives, to make sure you are not doubling up on medications. If you have acquired a puppy it is best to discuss the options with your vet when you are having your puppy vaccinated.

## Intestinal Worms

There are four main types of intestinal worms that are a major concern to dog owners. These are roundworms, hookworms, tapeworms, and whipworms. Control and prevention of intestinal worms is essential for maintenance of the health and well being of your dog. Your veterinarian can advise you on setting up a preventative worming regime. This involves worming your dog on a regular basis, such as every three months, without confirming that there are any worms present. If you prefer not to treat your dogs for worms that they may not actually have, it is essential that you get a faecal check done by your vet on a regular basis to screen for worms. Some worms have an environmental stage in their life cycle, so if you wait for symptoms to become apparent before treating your dog, or screening for worms, your yard can become heavily contaminated with worm eggs or larvae. This means that worms will be an ongoing problem for your dog and some types of worms can be transmitted to humans. In particular, children playing in the yard with the dog may be put at risk.

### Roundworms *(Toxocara canis & Toxascaris leonina)*

Probably the most common worm infestation found in dogs. They have a complex life cycle and are passed to unborn and nursing puppies, as well as dogs of all ages. It is believed that 70% of all pups are born with Toxocara canis, one of the two species of roundworms to infect dogs. Adult dogs become infected by either ingesting worm eggs from soil, or by eating another animal, such as a rat, that is infested with immature roundworms. The eggs need to develop in the environment for at least a month before they can infect an animal, so fresh faeces are not a threat if they are removed before they break down and contaminate the soil. Once ingested by a dog, the roundworms complete their life cycle inside the dog. If the dog is pregnant the third stage larvae migrate to the lungs of the unborn pups. If the dog is a lactating bitch, the third stage larvae migrate to the mammary glands and are passed in the milk to the puppies.

In all other ages the larvae migrate to the dog's lungs and are eventually coughed up and then swallowed, allowing them to enter the intestine again. Here they complete the fourth stage of their life cycle - mating and laying eggs that are passed in the dog's faeces.

**ROUNDWORM LIFE CYCLE**

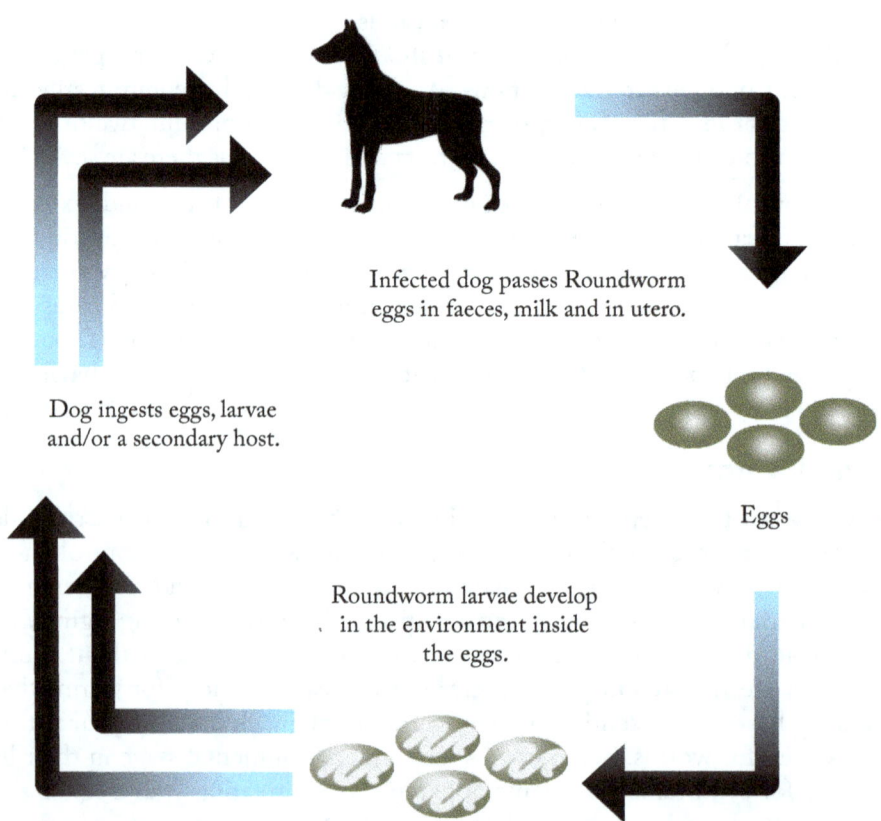

As roundworms rob the dog of nutrients, heavy infestations can result in loss of weight, poor condition, lethargy and a pot bellied appearance. Dogs can develop pneumonia due to the worms infecting the lungs and diarrhoea is common. Dogs may also vomit and large worms may be seen at this stage. Diagnosis is by symptoms and/or faecal testing. Due to the high infestation rate in puppies, most vets recommend a regular worming program for young dogs, without performing faecal checks. If your dog is not on a preventative program it is advisable to get a faecal check when you take your dog for its yearly veterinary check.

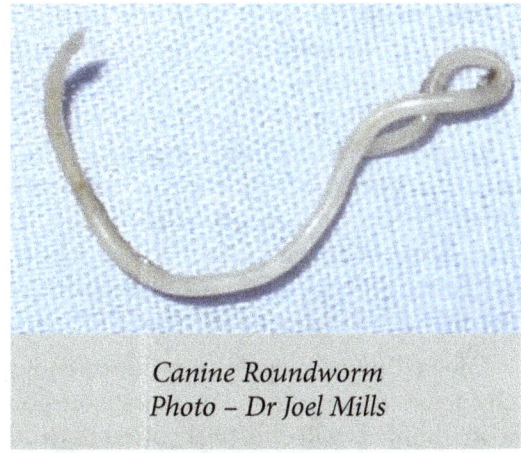

*Canine Roundworm*
*Photo – Dr Joel Mills*

The second species of roundworm, Toxascaris leonina, has a simpler life cycle. It completes its cycle in the intestine and does not migrate within the body. The same wormers are effective against both species. Many of the combination worming treatments are effective against roundworms. Monthly flea or heartworm prevention programs that include roundworm treatments are also effective in preventing environmental contamination. Due to the fact that roundworms can only be treated when they are present in the intestine, multiple treatments may be required to rid the dog's system of roundworms. The monthly preventative programs are effective in accomplishing this task.

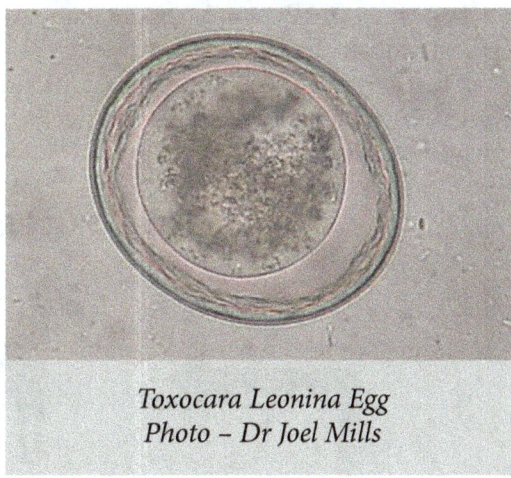

*Toxocara Leonina Egg*
*Photo – Dr Joel Mills*

## Hookworms (*Ancylostoma caninum, Ancylostoma braziliens*)

Heavy burdens of most intestinal worms can cause serious illness in your dog and hookworm, in particular, can cause death in young pups due to blood loss. Unlike other intestinal worms that absorb nutrients from food passing through the digestive system, hookworms suck blood directly from their host. Like roundworms they have an environmental stage in their life cycle and they can also migrate in the body, infecting the lungs and mammary glands as well as unborn puppies.

Hookworm eggs are passed into the environment through the droppings of infected dogs. The eggs hatch in the soil and complete two further stages of their life cycle before being able to infect another host. They do this in two ways- either by being licked up by a dog whose coat has been contaminated with soil carrying larvae, or by worms directly penetrating the skin when larvae come in contact with a potential host. It is important to note that worms may infect humans in this manner so children playing in areas where hookworm larvae are present are at risk of becoming infected, particularly through the soles of their feet.

Once the larvae are inside a new host they generally migrate to the intestine to complete their life cycle. Some however, migrate to other areas in the same manner as roundworms, infecting the lungs and trachea. Like roundworms they are eventually coughed up and swallowed, allowing them to complete the reproductive stage in the intestine. Some hookworms making this migration fail to complete the journey and become dormant in the body (encysted). These worms may become active again at a later time and are often activated by changes in the hormone levels of pregnant bitches. If they resume their migration at this time they are drawn to the unborn pups in the uterus and to the mammary glands. Pups are either born infected or become infected through the milk or through environmental contact with developing larvae.

Infected pups struggle to produce enough red blood cells to maintain growth and are characteristically pale and weak with on-going deficiencies. Many untreated pups with heavy worm burdens will effectively bleed to death. Worming products containing Mebendazole, Fenbendazole, or Pyrantel pamoate are used to treat infection but these are only effective against worms that are present in the GI tract. There is no treatment for encysted larvae in other parts of the body. Because of this, a second treatment is recommended thirty days later. Although treatment is effective, prevention of infection is desirable to reduce environmental contamination.

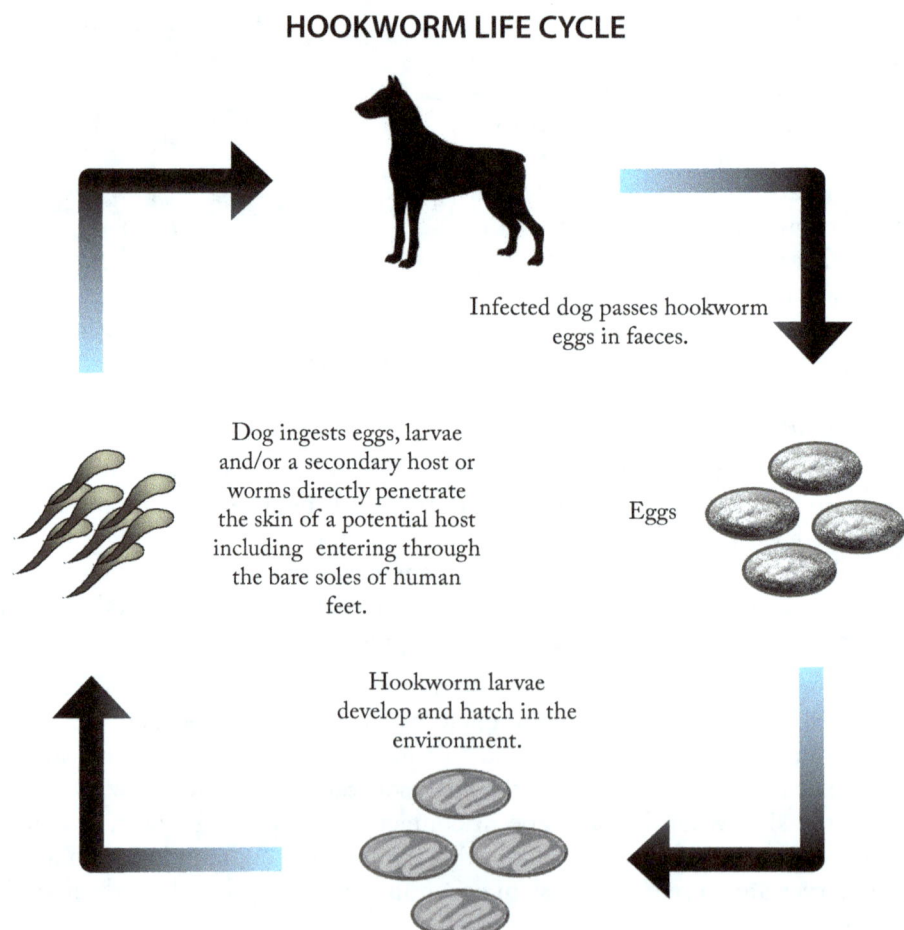

## Whipworms *(Trichuris vulpis)*

Adult whipworms embed themselves in the walls of the large intestine where they suck blood and lay eggs. The eggs are passed in the faeces and must remain in the environment for two to four weeks to complete part of their life cycle before they can infect a new host. This means that contaminated soil becomes the source of infection, not fresh droppings. Soil can remain contaminated with whipworm eggs for years so prevention is desirable. Eggs are ingested by the new host where they hatch in the small intestine before moving to the large intestine to complete their life cycle.

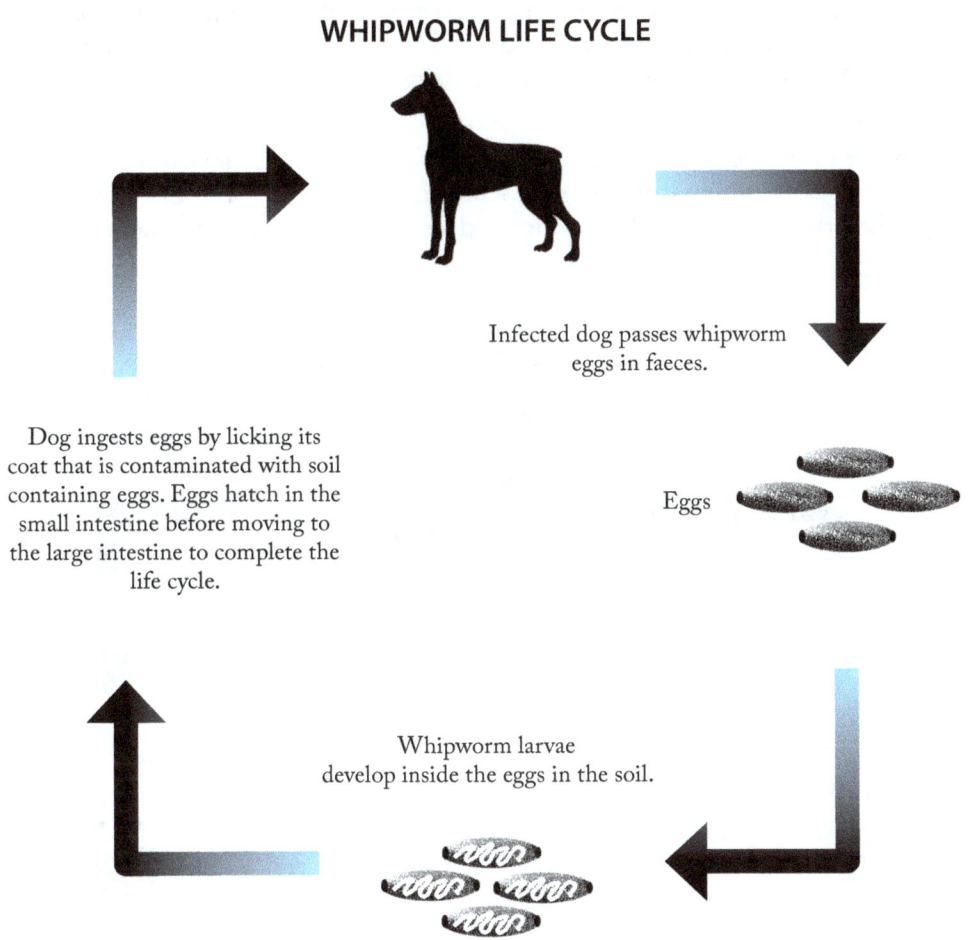

**WHIPWORM LIFE CYCLE**

Infected dog passes whipworm eggs in faeces.

Eggs

Whipworm larvae develop inside the eggs in the soil.

Dog ingests eggs by licking its coat that is contaminated with soil containing eggs. Eggs hatch in the small intestine before moving to the large intestine to complete the life cycle.

Inflammation, diarrhoea and bleeding in the large intestine can result from heavy burdens of whipworms. The blood loss is generally not significant enough to be dangerous but the diarrhoea can become chronic. Heavy burdens can also result in intermittent symptoms of weakness and dehydration that mimic Addison's disease.

Most combination worming agents are not effective against whipworms and they can be difficult to detect in faecal tests. Therefore treatment is often based on symptoms. Some heartworm prevention medications have now been developed to also control and treat whipworms. Your vet will be able to advise you on a suitable product that is available in your area.

## Tapeworms *(Dipylidium caninum)*

These are the least harmful of the intestinal worms and easily prevented if you keep your dog free of fleas. They rely on fleas to be able to complete their life cycle. These worms get their name from the fact that they are flat in appearance, resembling a piece of white tape. An adult tapeworm can be as much as six inches long but it is made up of many small segments that are attached to the head which embeds itself in the wall of the small intestine.

Each segment has its own digestive system and new segments are produced behind the head. Older segments move down the line and by the time they become the last segment, their only function is reproduction. When these segments drop off they are full of tapeworm eggs. The egg sacks are passed in faeces but some may remain around the dog's anus. The egg sack is able to move but eventually breaks open scattering tapeworm eggs in the dog's coat and bedding.

Foraging flea larvae eat the eggs. During the course of normal grooming, the dog then swallows the fleas carrying tapeworm eggs while licking its coat. The tapeworm eggs infect the dog when the body of the flea is digested releasing the eggs into the dog's digestive system.

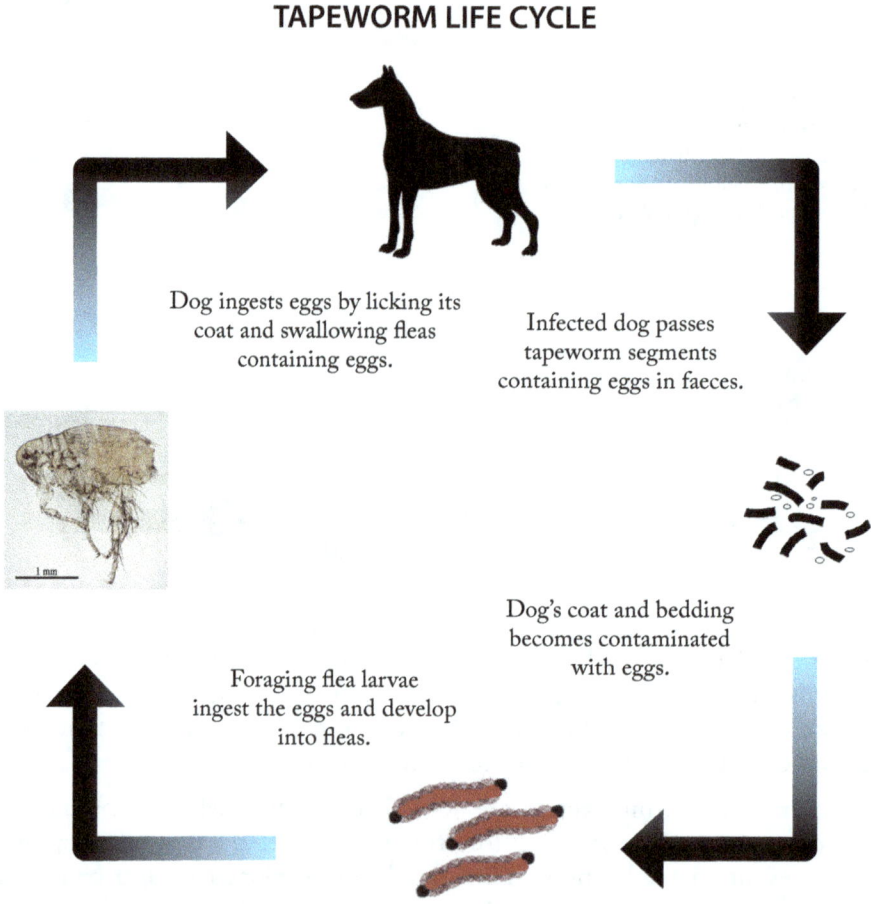

**TAPEWORM LIFE CYCLE**

Dog ingests eggs by licking its coat and swallowing fleas containing eggs.

Infected dog passes tapeworm segments containing eggs in faeces.

Dog's coat and bedding becomes contaminated with eggs.

Foraging flea larvae ingest the eggs and develop into fleas.

Although not particularly harmful, it is best to rid the dog of tapeworms if detected. Diagnosis is generally based on sighting worm segments in the dog's droppings and treatment for tapeworms is with medication containing Praziquantel. Breaking the flea cycle is obviously the best prevention for this parasite.

## Hydatid Tapeworms *(Echinococcus granulosis)*

This is one of seven species of tapeworm that can infect dogs in Australia. It is also common southern South America, the southern and central Russia, East Africa, and the western United States. Dogs become infected primarily through eating the offal of sheep, cattle and kangaroos. These animals may carry cysts containing hydatid eggs, so farm dogs are most at risk. Infection is common in wild dogs and dingoes and these can be infected with thousands of hydatids while remaining reasonably healthy. They are much smaller than the more common tapeworm seen in dogs and segments cannot be detected visually in the dog's droppings.

Although the infection causes minimal problems in dogs, the main concern with hydatids is that the infection is much more serious in humans. Humans may become infected by contact with their dogs, inadvertently swallowing microscopic eggs. The dogs coat may be contaminated with sticky hydatid eggs passed in the dog's droppings, so washing hands after handling your dog is particularly important in high risk areas. In humans, the infection results in watery cysts that can form anywhere in the body including the brain. While infection can be treated with a worming agent in dogs, in humans, surgery is required to remove the cysts. Depending on the size and the location of the cyst, surgery can carry high risk. Feeding only canned and dry dog food can prevent infection and regular worming with Praziquantel is recommended for dogs in high risk situations.

## Fleas

If your dog begins scratching or appears to be developing a skin irritation, it may have fleas. To check for fleas comb through your dogs coat with a fine toothed comb. Shake out any bits of 'grit' or 'dirt' that are collected on the comb onto a piece of white paper and then wet the paper. If any of these bits look red or stain the paper red once wet, it is very likely that they are flea droppings including digested dog blood.

Fleas are not caused by poor hygiene – they occur naturally in the environment and can affect dogs from all walks of life! They can be a major problem if left untreated as the dog may develop anaemia, flea bite allergies, dermatitis, skin infections from bacteria that colonise the damaged area, and tapeworm infestations as fleas are part of the tapeworm life cycle. The important thing to know about flea allergies is the dog only needs to be bitten once to develop an allergic reaction – it does not need to be infested by fleas! The good news is they are easily controlled by following a flea eradication program recommended by your veterinarian. What is important to keep in mind is that part of the life cycle of the flea is spent off the dog. Therefore, to break the life cycle of fleas, it is vitally important that you treat the environmental stage as well. The following diagram demonstrates the importance of environmental control due to the fact that worm eggs account for the largest proportion of the infestation.

There is a confusing array of flea products available on the market today and new, more "user friendly" products are appearing constantly. It is best not to buy the cheap alternatives from the supermarket. A product from your vet that will be effective on the environment as well as the dog is definitely worth paying a little bit more for. Flea treatments are insecticides that can cause toxicity if not used correctly – ALWAYS follow the directions and keep them safely stored away from your pets and children. Never use products designed for use on cats – dogs and cats react very differently to chemicals.

Never use insecticides that are out of date, as they can become very toxic. Signs of insecticide poisoning can include salivation, depression, laboured breathing, muscle spasms, weakness and convulsions. Always take extra care when treating young pups, pregnant dogs or debilitated or elderly dogs and observe your dog closely after treatment. Consult your vet and follow their advice if you suspect poisoning.

## FLEA LIFE CYCLE

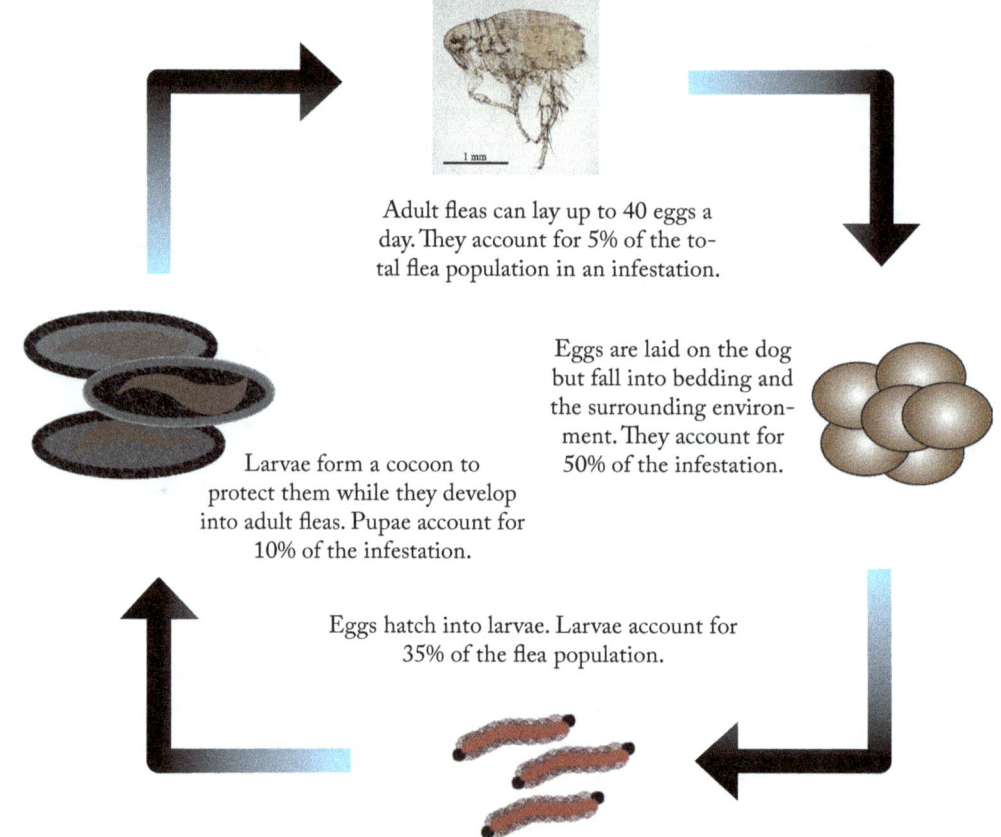

Adult fleas can lay up to 40 eggs a day. They account for 5% of the total flea population in an infestation.

Eggs are laid on the dog but fall into bedding and the surrounding environment. They account for 50% of the infestation.

Larvae form a cocoon to protect them while they develop into adult fleas. Pupae account for 10% of the infestation.

Eggs hatch into larvae. Larvae account for 35% of the flea population.

Flea treatment/control products are generally grouped as follows;

**Collars:** The most effective of these contain Insect Growth Regulators (IGR) - These produce a hormone that prevents fleas from developing into adults capable of reproduction. They will not kill adult fleas but are effecting in interfering with the life cycle of fleas. Flea collars are not effective when used alone.

**Topical Flea Adulticides:** These products are applied as a small pre-measured dose to the skin in an area that the dog cannot reach, such as between the shoulders at the base of the neck. They spread over the dog's skin within 24 hours, killing adult fleas. They do not include chemicals designed to interfere with the life cycle of fleas so they can be used in conjunction with IGR collars as an effective total eradication regime.

**Oral Treatments:** Like collars, these contain Insect Growth Regulators to help break the life cycle of fleas. Protection usually lasts 30 days.

**Broad Spectrum Treatments:** These are becoming the most popular safe method of controlling both internal and external parasites. Some brands are effective against a number of intestinal worms as well as heartworm, several species of skin mites, and both immature and mature fleas and ticks, though their effectiveness against ticks may not extend for as long as the flea protection. Some broad spectrum treatments are oral while others are topical.

There are other shampoos, sprays, adulticide collars and herbal remedies. While these can be effective in killing adult fleas, they do not address the life cycle of the flea and therefore the long term success is limited in comparison to the newer products mentioned above. Always read the label, check the use by date, and follow instructions to the letter. Used correctly, modern flea treatments will do their job without stressing your dog or yourself. If you have any concerns about potential allergies that you dog may have to flea treatments it is best to consult your veterinarian.

## Ticks

There are a number of different species of ticks, all of which feed on the blood of their host. Some just engorge themselves with blood and then drop off leaving a small inflamed area, while others can cause serious, life threatening illness in the dogs they feed on.

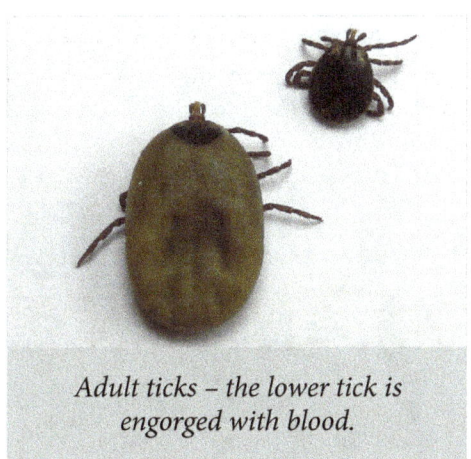

*Adult ticks – the lower tick is engorged with blood.*

Ticks have four stages in their life cycle. While some species complete their whole life cycle on one host, others may drop off one animal and complete their life cycle on another. It is these ticks that are capable of carrying and transmitting viruses that can spread diseases such as Lyme's Disease from one infected animal to another. Health issues can vary depending on the regional area that the ticks inhabit. Ticks in some areas can cause paralysis, rickettsial disease, bacterial and viral disease and Babesiosis, caused by a parasite that infects red blood cells.

Your local vet is the best person to speak to regarding the risks of tick infection. Grooming and careful observation is the best way of detecting ticks in dogs that are at risk. There are some preventative treatments available but these should be discussed with your vet as they may not be required in a low risk area. Because of the health issues associated with some ticks, most vets recommend the immediate removal of ticks. The most effective method of achieving this is holding the tick by the head, close to the body, with a pair of tweezers and pulling it straight out without twisting. Topical insecticides that protect against ticks will also be effective but will take longer.

## Mites

Mite infestation is much less common in dogs than fleas but there are three mite infestations that are cause for concern and will usually require veterinary attention.

## Demodex mites

These are common in small numbers on dogs and rarely cause a noticeable problem. They are passed onto pups at an early age from their nursing mothers. In some susceptible dogs the numbers can increase dramatically causing localised bald patches around the face and front legs. These patches can sometimes become infected with bacteria resulting in serious illness. It is believed that this Demodectic Mange may only occur in immuno-suppressed animals and there may be a genetic factor involved that compromises the immune system. As a result, dogs with recurring problems with this mite are often recommended to be sterilised.

## Sarcoptes mites

Although rare, can cause itchiness and crusty lesions in both humans and dogs. The active infestation is known as Sarcoptic Mange and can be treated topically or with injectable insecticides.

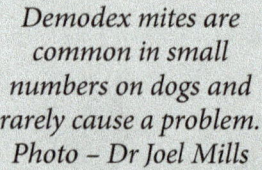
*Demodex mites are common in small numbers on dogs and rarely cause a problem. Photo – Dr Joel Mills*

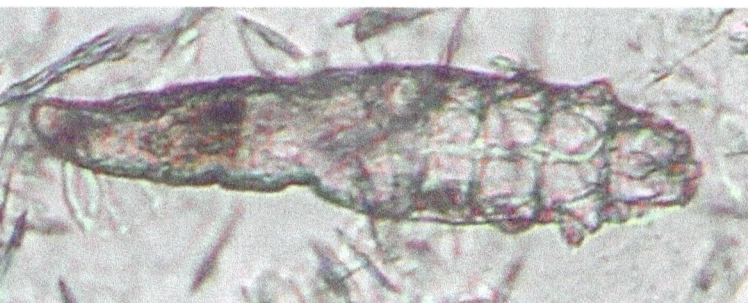

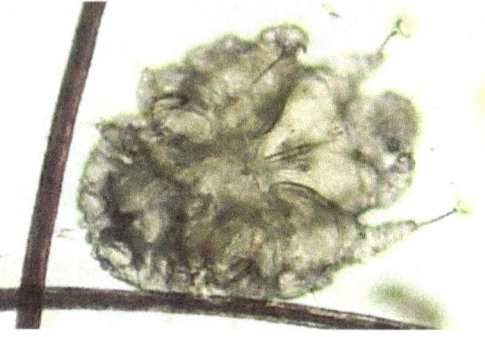
*Sarcoptes mites (left) are rare but cause inflammatory responses and should be treated. Photos – Dr Joel Mills*

## Ear Mites

These mites are considered a rare infection amongst dogs but can be transmitted from one dog to the next by direct physical contact. They cause an inflammatory response and a characteristic black waxy discharge in the ears. The condition may be diagnosed by a vet based on the discharge alone but also through microscopic examination of the ear wax. The infection is treated topically and all pets in the household will need to be treated. Ear mites are not transmitted to humans.

# Teeth and Nails

## Dental Care

Preventing the deterioration of your dog's teeth is important for the long-term health of your dog. Teeth that are allowed to become encrusted with tartar and gums that become inflamed, are painful and result in bad breath, inappetence, and can eventually lead to serious health issues involving other vital organs such as the heart valves and kidneys. Serious pathogenic bacteria from infected teeth and gums may enter the bloodstream where they are transported to other parts of the body causing serious damage.

The health of your dog's teeth can be maintained through the use of appropriate dental chews and diet. Due to the abrasive effects of feeding dry food, these diets can help reduce the likelihood of periodontal disease. Rawhide chews, raw bones in moderation, and special dental chews can all help exercise the gums and remove plaques. If you are unable to keep your dog's teeth from developing tartar through these methods you can also help to keep your dog's teeth in good shape through brushing. By conditioning your dog from an early age to allow its teeth to be brushed, you can help remove plaque before it develops into bacteria-harbouring tartar. With lots of positive reinforcement training, this need not be traumatic. It is important not to make it a negative experience, resulting in resentment, as there are other alternatives if your dog strongly objects to brushing. Only edible toothpaste, especially made for dogs should be used with either a special dog toothbrush or a finger brush. Human toothpaste is not meant to be swallowed but it is unlikely that even the cleverest dog will master the

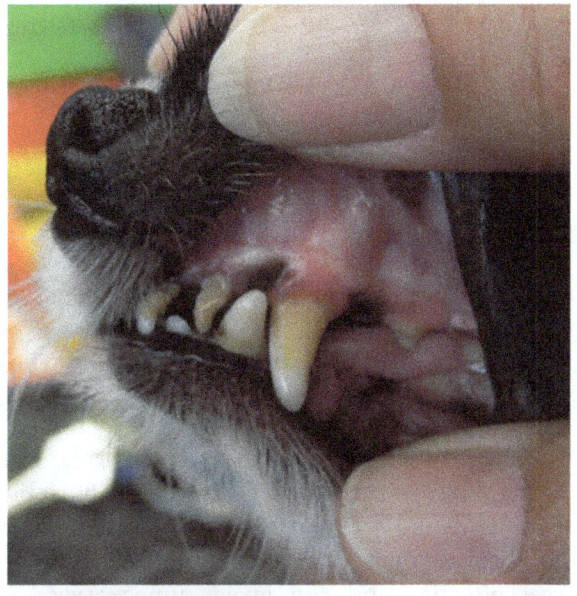

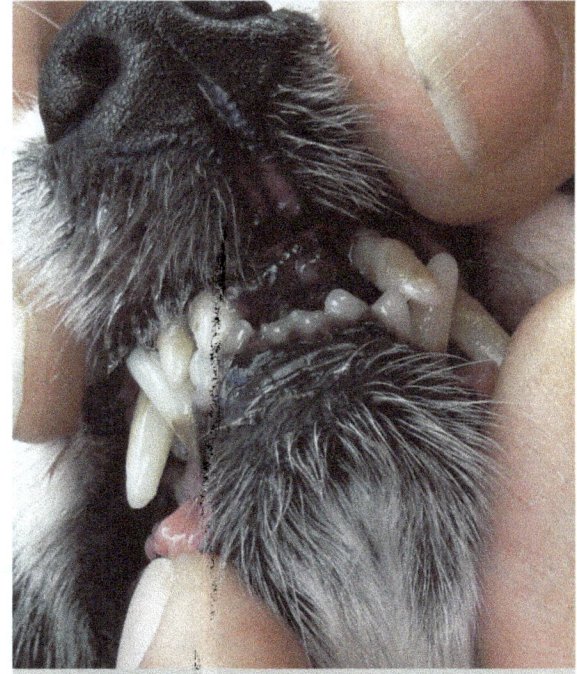

*Teeth that are allowed to become encrusted with tartar and gums that become inflamed, are painful and result in bad breath, inappetence, and can eventually lead to serious health issues.*

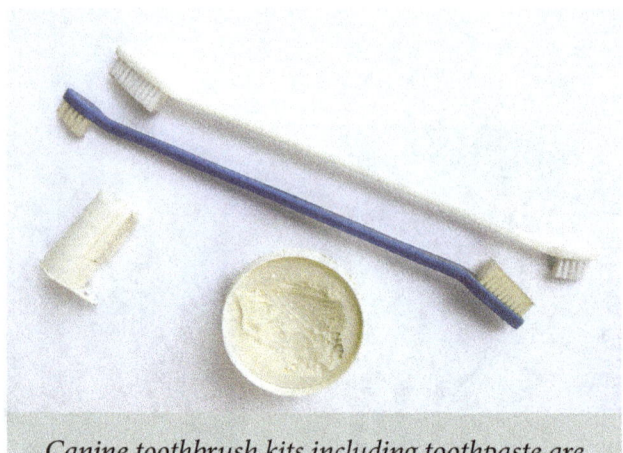

*Canine toothbrush kits including toothpaste are generally available from vets and some pet stores.*

rinse and spit procedure needed with human toothpaste. Most vet nurses or technicians will happily spend some time with you demonstrating how to brush your dog's teeth, usually as part of the 'over the counter service'.

Once plaques have developed into hard brown tartar deposits they can no longer be removed by brushing but early intervention by a veterinarian can help remove these before more serious damage to the teeth occurs and infection results. Signs of early periodontal disease include redness of the gums, foul smelling breath and brown tartar deposits. Remember that a dog with a painful mouth is less likely to eat well but is more likely to bite as a result of the pain it is experiencing. Serious dental work will require a general anaesthetic and can be very costly. An early preventative dental care program is far more cost effective and can avoid unnecessary suffering in your dog.

*Appropriate dental chews can help keep a dog's teeth in good condition.*

*With behavioural conditioning your dog can learn to accept regular brushing.*

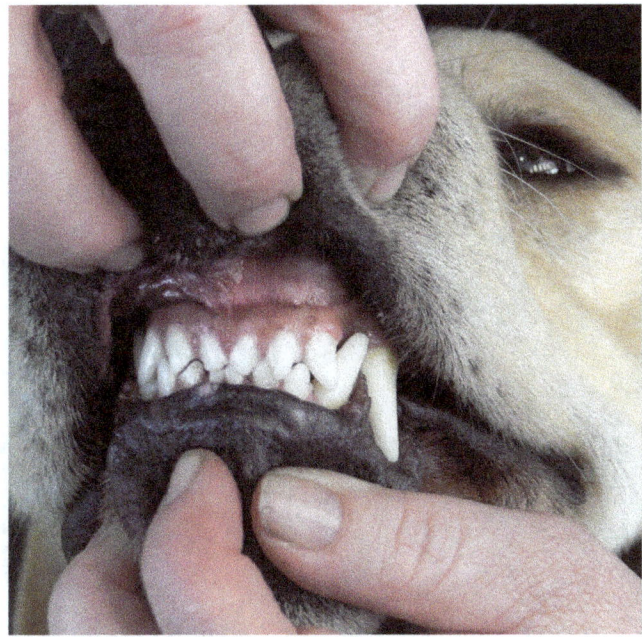

*Healthy white teeth and clean pink gums in a young Labrador.*

## Nail Trimming

Like dental care, trimming your dog's nails is also important for the overall, long term health of your dog. Nails that are left untrimmed can split, break and bleed, causing soreness in the dog's feet and toes, and possible infection. Toenails can sometimes grow so long that they can curl backwards, penetrating the dog's pads.

The requirement for nail trimming can vary depending on the breed of dog, its age, its level of exercise and the environment in which the dog is kept. Working and herding breeds are active and generally have compact feet with well arched toes that angle the toenails downwards towards the ground (often referred to as 'cat feet'). If these dogs are active on hard surfaces such as gravel, rock and concrete, their nails may not need trimming until they slow down with age and exercise less. Small dogs, dogs that receive low levels of exercise and those that spend a lot of time on grass and other soft substrate may need to have their nails trimmed at an early age. Breeds that are inclined to be 'hare' footed (long hare-like feet that encourage nails to grow more forward than downward) are also likely to develop long nails. If you notice a change in the sound of your dogs nails on hard floors they may require trimming.

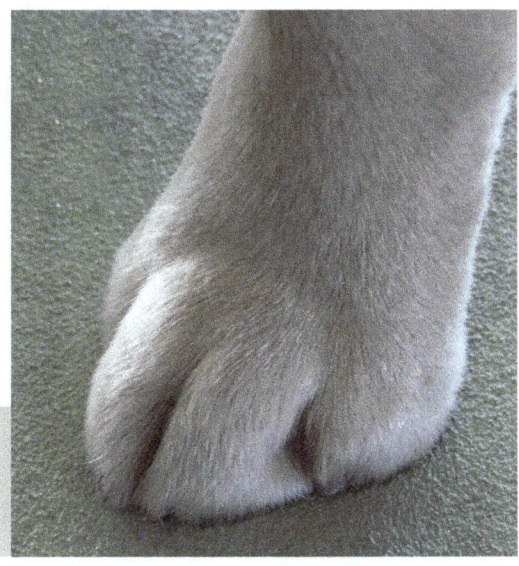

*Breeds with compact feet and well arched toes that are active on hard surfaces may not require frequent trimming.*

Through positive reinforcement training, dogs can be desensitised to having their nails trimmed so that the procedure need not be a traumatic experience. Many people prefer to have the vet trim their dog's nails but if regular trimming is required it is best to learn how to safely do the procedure yourself so that the nails do not get too long between vet visits. The longer the nails are left to grow without trimming, the harder it is to bring them back to a reasonable length as the 'quick' (the blood vessel that feeds the growing nail) grows long in proportion to the nail and will bleed if cut. Trimming long nails on a weekly basis will help bring them back under control as the 'quick' will retreat into the nail, allowing each cut to shorten the nail until they reach normal length again.

It is advisable to get your vet or an experienced dog groomer to demonstrate how to safely trim your dog's nails. A good quality pair of dog nail clippers is required. Nails need to be trimmed from the back at a 45° angle towards the point of the nail. Multiple small cuts should be made to avoid taking too much at once, inflicting pain and causing the nail to bleed. As you approach the end of the quick, the nail will darken in the centre in black nails, and a deeper pink shade will appear in white nails. If the nail splinters, the rough edges should be filed smooth by filing gently from the back to the front. Much praise should be given during the procedure and frequent rests taken if the dog finds the procedure stressful.

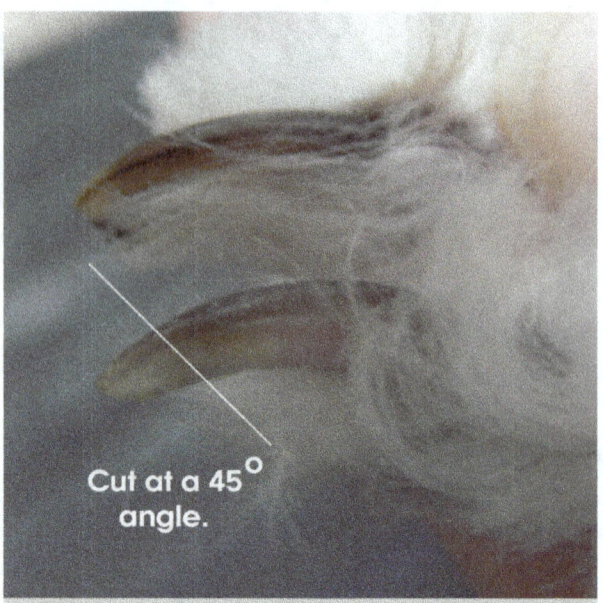

*Nails need to be trimmed from the back at a 45° angle towards the point of the nail.*

*Nails should clipped at a 45° angle, a small amount at a time to avoid bleeding from the 'quick'.*

If you are going to attempt to clip your dog's nails it is advisable to have something on hand to stop the bleeding in case you accidentally cut the 'quick'. Products such as ferric chloride or potassium permanganate (bought over the counter from a human pharmacy) are useful. Applying the solution or crystals to the bleeding nail with cotton wool will cause the blood to clot quickly. Many human first aid kits also contain a styptic (blood clotting material) that looks a little like orange cotton wool. This can also be applied to the bleeding nail. In cases where a dog has unexpectedly damaged a nail and none of these products are on hand, pressure can be applied to the tip to stop the bleeding, or the tip of the nail can be scraped along a bar of softened soap to plug the end of the nail. This should only be attempted if the tip alone is damaged and the injury is not extensive. If the latter is the case, seek the advice of a veterinarian.

## Grooming

### Brushing and Trimming

The necessity for grooming will vary tremendously depending on the lifestyle that you enjoy with your dog and the type of coat that your dog has. You should not consider a long haired breed if you do not have the time to make a regular commitment to grooming or the funds to pay someone else to do it for you on a regular basis. Short and wire haired breeds make life a lot easier but these dogs still require regular grooming to keep them clean and to keep their coats in good condition. Grooming stimulates the production of oil in the dog's coat, keeping it shiny and helping to prevent it from becoming dry and brittle.

There are other benefits of grooming your dog that should be considered. Most dogs enjoy grooming. It is an integral part of bonding with your dog and reassures their sense of belonging to a pack. In the wild, wolves and other wild dogs clean each others ears, eyes and faces by licking one another. Dogs also groom themselves by licking, but giving them a helping hand is usually greatly appreciated. It is an extension of stroking and is also the best way to recognise any lumps and bumps, grass seeds, rashes, and wounds that may need attention. The other thing to consider is that the more hair that you remove through brushing outside, the less hair you have to

*Most dogs enjoy being groomed once they are accustomed to it.*

contend with on your clothing, floor, and furniture. This is particularly important when dogs are shedding their coats during a moult. If the shedding is allowed to progress at its own pace, which can take several weeks, large drifts of hair can rapidly accumulate in the house. Brushing can remove the dead hair much more rapidly and the sooner it is gone the sooner your dog will be back to looking its best.

Long or short haired, the more often you groom your dog the better. However, long haired breeds will benefit most from a daily brush to avoid hair mats forming that can be difficult to remove. Often when severe mats form, the only solution is to cut them out, resulting in a typical moth eaten appearance. It may be safer to enlist the help of a vet or professional groomer to remove severe mats to avoid accidentally cutting the skin. Smaller mats can be teased out with slicker brushes or mat breakers but this can sometimes be very time consuming and uncomfortable for the dog. In the long run you may save yourself more time by dedicating a short time each day, or at least several times a week, to grooming a long haired dog. Tangle free sprays may make the task of removing mats easier. Wire haired breeds, such as many of the Terriers, need to have hair around their eyes clipped regularly to prevent discharge from their eyes building up.

For most coats you should brush in the direction of the hair beginning with the head, shoulders, and neck, working down the body to the legs and to the tail. With long coarse coats that have a soft short undercoat, and short coarse Terrier coats, the undercoat can be brushed against the grain to help

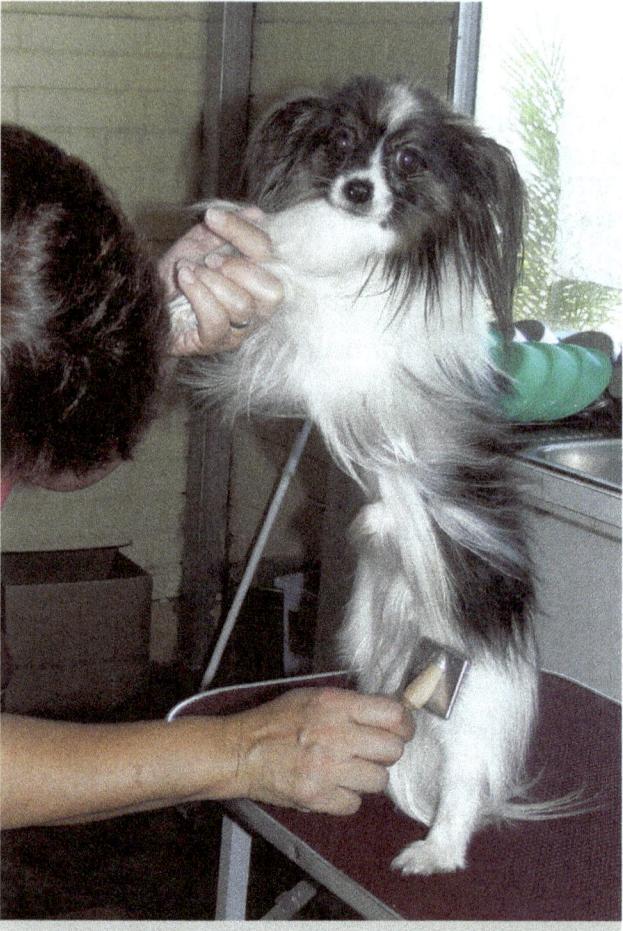

*For most coats you should brush in the direction of the hair, working down the body to the legs and to the tail.*

lift and fluff the coat before brushing the top coat with the direction of the hair. With long coats it is best to divide the coat into sections and brush from the skin out. Some groomers use rubber bands and clips to hold sections of hair out of the way while they complete another section, helping them to make sure that each section is free of tangles.

There are many different brushes and combs and grooming tools on the market that have different purposes. Here are some recommendations;

## Bristle Brushes

Generally available in soft, medium, and firm. Soft to medium are generally used for soft coats. Short closely spaced bristles are used for soft, short coats and wider spaced, longer bristles used on soft long coats. Firmer bristle brushes are used for wire coats, such as Terrier coats, and long coats that have a coarse outer coat, such as Collies and Old English Sheepdogs. Again, short closely spaced bristles are used on the shorter coats and longer wider bristles are used for the long coarse coats.

## Wire Pin Brushes

Most often used for long fine or coarse coats. They are useful for removing dead undercoat, particularly when moulting.

*Bristle brushes are generally available in soft, medium, and firm.*

*Pin Brushes come in a variety of pin lengths. The pins on good quality pin brushes are polished to avoid scratching.*

## Combs

Generally used after brushing to remove more dead and loose hair. Many have wider pins at one end and closer pins at the other end. Always begin by using the wider end of the comb to avoid pulling out hair if you hit a tangle that hasn't been removed by brushing.

## Slicker Brushes

These have short fine metal teeth that are useful for teasing out mats. The idea is to break up mats that involve the outer coat first before tackling mats that are close to the skin involving the undercoat.

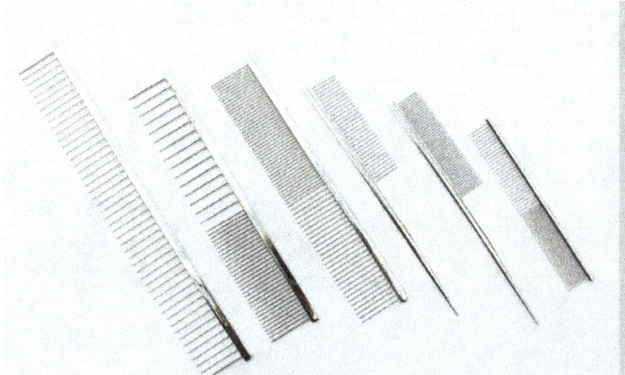

*Combs come in a variety of widths.*

# Mat Breakers, De-matting Combs, Stripping Combs or Knives, and Coat Rakes

These may have replaceable blades and are designed to help break up hair mats so that they can be more easily removed. These are also used to thin the coats of some wire haired breeds, such as the Airedale Terrier, and dogs that have their body haired thinned along their backs for the showring, such as Schnauzers and West Highland White Terriers. It is best to have these demonstrated by an experienced groomer as removing hair mats and stripping the coat can cause damage to the coat and be painful to the dog, if not done properly. Undercoat rakes are designed to penetrate the outer coat without damage to remove dead hair from the undercoat.

*De-matting combs, below top, also referred to as 'mat breakers' are used for breaking up large mats. Stripping combs, below bottom, are used for thinning the coat.*

*Slicker brushes are useful for teasing out mats.*

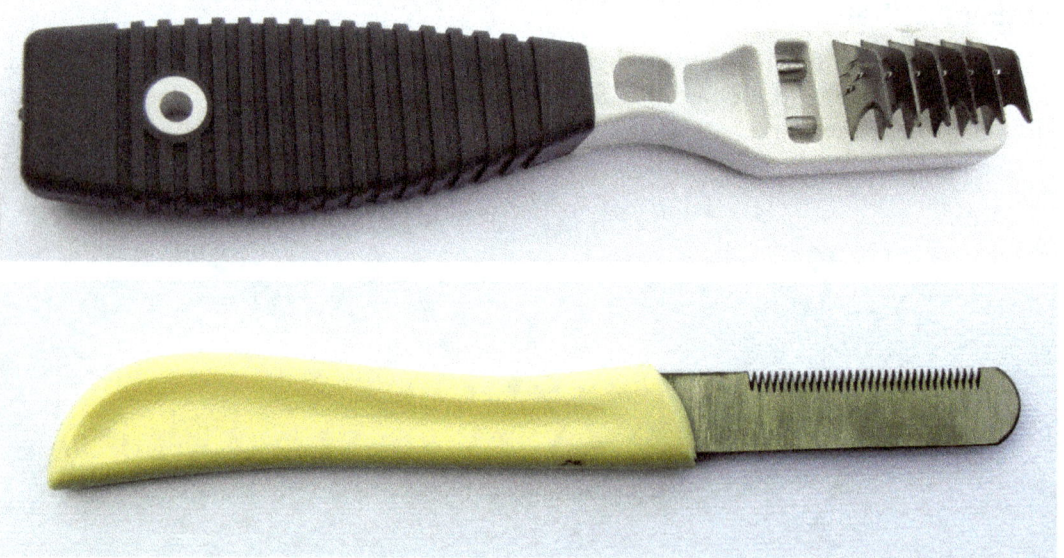

## Scissors and Clippers

Like professional hairdressers, people who groom dogs professionally generally use expensive, top quality scissors and clippers in order to cut and shape the coat to an even finish without damage. If your dog requires regular clipping you may want to invest in some good equipment and learn to clip and trim properly. There are videos and books available to help you learn. If less frequent clipping is required it may be better to leave it to a professional. Shaving is not recommended for most breeds as it removes the undercoat which many breeds rely on for insulation. It also exposes the dog's skin to sunburn.

## Rubber Brushes and Grooming Mitts

These brushes do not have bristles but have raised rubber nodules instead. They are most suited to very smooth coated dogs and are effective at grabbing dead hair and removing it from the coat. Some owners use them on wet dogs to remove the dead hair loosened during their bath. The mitts are particularly good if your dog is nervous about brushes as it is a more subtle transition from stroking to brushing.

*Coat King™ grooming rakes, far left, also classified as 'mat breakers', are used for breaking up large mats and removing dead hair. Undercoat rakes, left, are useful for removing dead hair from the undercoat.*

*Above - Rubber brush and grooming mitt.*

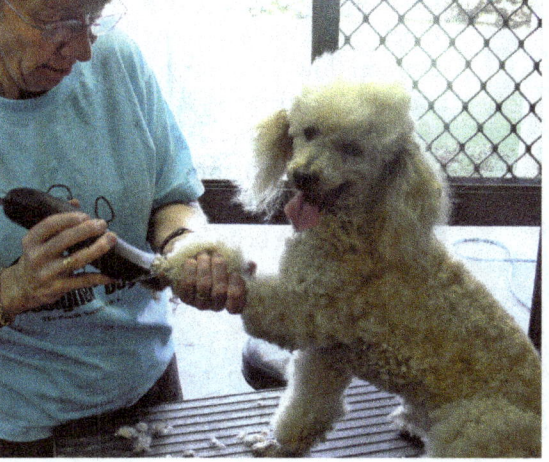

*Left - Clipping may be best left to a professional dog groomer.*

## Bathing

There are no hard and fast rules regarding how often you bath your dog. For dogs, it is a natural instinct to roll in things that smell really awful to disguise their own scent. As a result, bathing will usually be an unavoidable task from time to time. Providing that you use shampoos and conditioners that have been formulated for dogs, and that your dog is not allergic to the ingredients in your shampoo, bathing can be as frequent as you require. However, bath time is not an enjoyable experience for many dogs, so inflicting too many bath sessions on your dog is likely to result in some resentment. If your dog's coat is kept clean from brushing, less bathing is required and this will help preserve the natural oils in the dog's coat. This is probably preferable to frequent baths, particularly from your dog's point of view! Insecticide shampoos should only be used if necessary, as these tend to dry out the skin more than normal shampoos.

It is important to brush out and remove any hair mats before bathing your dog as they will only get worse and harder to remove after washing. Most dogs that have not been washed for some time will require at least two applications of shampoo, with a rinse in between, to adequately clean the coat. If your dog has an undercoat, it is difficult with the first shampoo to get the dog thoroughly wet as the undercoat is full of oil and is very water repellent. The first shampoo will break down the oils and allow the second shampoo to penetrate the undercoat and remove more dirt and oil. Make sure the water is not too hot (lukewarm is best) and it is important to be thorough in rinsing the soap out of the dog's coat. Soap left in the coat may cause skin irritations.

Instinctively, your dog will shake vigorously to remove excess water from its coat which usually leaves the handler almost as wet as the dog. The drying process can be sped up by towelling the dog, a process which most dogs seem to derive a great deal of pleasure from. Rub the towel along the dog's body with the grain of the coat to remove excess water, and then rub vigorously against the grain to help remove more water.

*Bath time is not an enjoyable experience for many dogs, so inflicting too many baths on your dog is likely to result in some resentment.*

You need to be careful with long haired dogs not to create too many tangles with towel drying. It is best to comb out tangles while the coat is still wet. Even short to medium coats will dry looking better with a brush after towelling to put the hair back where it belongs. A blow dryer can also be used on low heat and is particularly effective in lifting and fluffing the coat of long haired breeds. It is important to remember that once the undercoat is wet it may take a long time to dry fully. Dogs can become very cold unless they have somewhere warm to dry off. Exercising your dog while it dries is a good way to keep it warm, but you need to be ready to stop it rolling in the dirt as this is instinctive behaviour for a wet dog.

## Ear Cleaning

Keeping ears clean is important for all dogs but more so for dogs that have long hair, ears that hang down, or a combination of both. Long haired breeds often suffer ear infections as a result of having a lot of hair growing inside their ears. The hair traps moisture and provides an ideal environment for bacterial and fungal infections to develop.

Clipping or pulling ear hairs is recommended for these dogs though the latter may result in some resentment. A vet or professional groomer should demonstrate ear hair removal for you before you attempt this yourself. Long folded ears also trap moisture and need regular cleaning even if they are free of hair.

Removal of excess ear hair can be made simpler by applying a small amount of special powder to the inside of the ear. The powder makes gripping the hair much easier but before you start dumping powder in your dog's ear, or poking around with a cotton bud, you should be aware that ears are sensitive organs that are easily damaged. The consequences of damaging the inside of the ear are serious. Without a demonstration by a vet or professional groomer, it is best to go no further than cleaning the outer, easily accessed areas of the ear cavity with a cotton ball, swab or tissue soaked in an ear cleaner suitable for dogs. These ear cleaning solutions or special ear wipes are available from pet shops or vets. Never apply ear medication solutions, such as antibacterial, antifungal or anti parasite to your dogs ear without a veterinary ear examination first. If the inner ear canal is ruptured or inflamed, you can cause severe damage and pain.

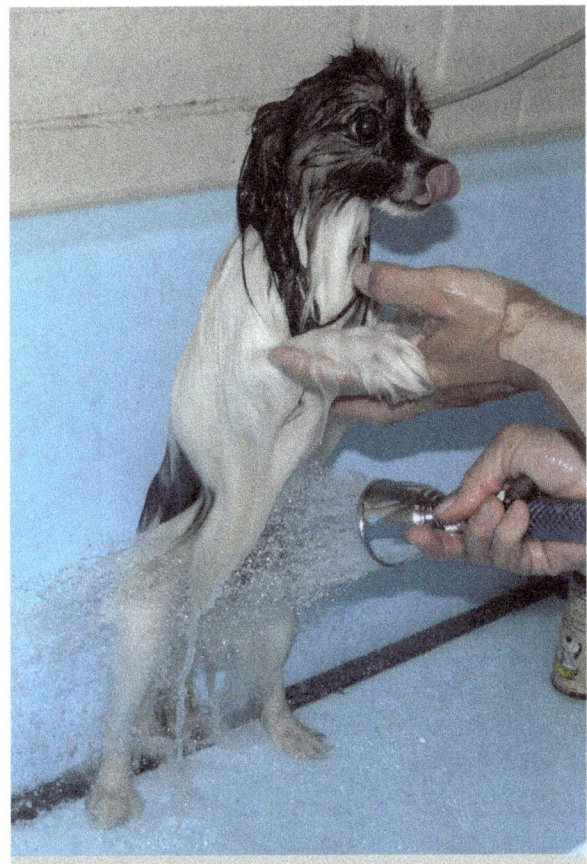

*It is important to be thorough in rinsing the soap out of the dog's coat.*

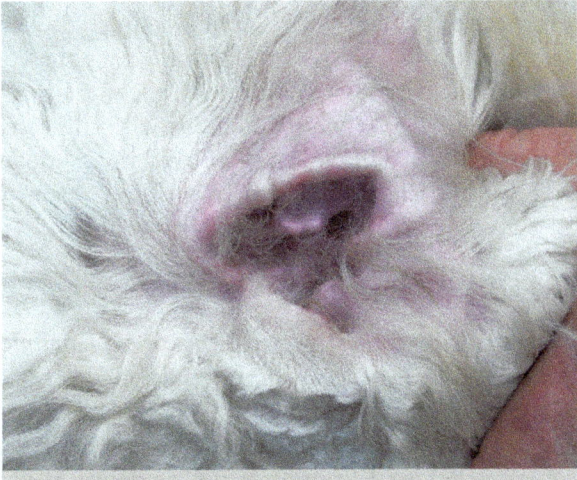

*This clean healthy poodle ear has some inner hair that will need to be regularly removed to maintain the cleanliness of the ear.*

## Anal Glands

Many people are unaware that a dog has anal glands, and that these may sometimes cause problems. However, they may have witnessed a dog dragging its bottom along the ground and been unsure of the cause. This behaviour, often referred to as scooting, is often incorrectly attributed to worm infestation. Although worm infestation may contribute to, and aggravate the condition, it is not the direct cause.

Dogs have anal glands, also referred to as anal sacs, on either side of the anus just inside the opening. They excrete a strong and unpleasant odour, in the form of a thick discharge, used to mark the dog's territory in the wild. Domestic dogs have lost the ability to empty the glands voluntarily. As a result, in some dogs the glands can become impacted. This impaction can be very uncomfortable and can result in a painful abscess forming. The dog scoots its bottom along the ground in an effort to empty the glands. They may also lick their anus obsessively, or chase their tail.

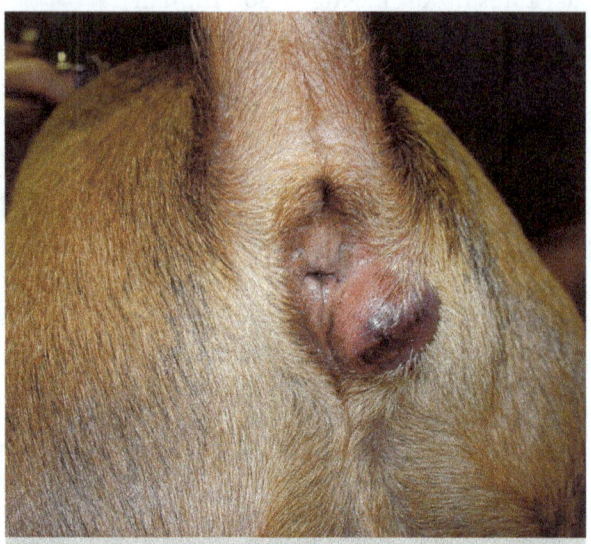

*Failure to empty impacted anal sacs can result in a painful abscess forming. Photo – Dr Joel Mills*

Exercise and high fibre diets that produce bulkier faeces are thought to help in preventing the anal sacs from becoming impacted. If impaction does occur, the glands may need to be emptied manually. This is a fairly simple procedure that can be easily learned, but the prospect of dealing with a foul smelling discharge and the rear end of a dog sends most people scurrying to the vet. In some dogs the condition reoccurs frequently and therefore, having your vet demonstrate the procedure may be helpful from a financial point of view. Dogs that have frequent problems with impacted anal glands can also undergo surgery to remove the anal glands. This procedure is known as an anal sacculectomy and does carry the risk of damage to nerves in the anal area. If you are contemplating surgery you should discuss the procedure in detail with your vet.

## Sterilisation

You might wonder why sterilisation is included in a chapter called 'Keeping Your Dog Healthy'. The process, referred to as 'neutering' for males and 'spaying' for females, is not simply a surgical procedure that prevents a dog from reproducing. It is also considered to have some long term health benefits as well. In males, the veterinarian removes the testicles, which is believed to reduce the incidence of prostate problems and eliminate the risk of testicular cancer. In females the uterus and ovaries are removed, reducing the likelihood of mammary gland tumours. A common problem in females that have not been sterilised is known as 'pyometra', which causes a serious infection of the uterus. Spaying will also avoid uterine cancer. However, there is also growing evidence that there are some health risks associated with these procedures, particularly for male dogs, that should be taken into consideration when deciding when to have your dog sterilised.

Studies suggest that the absence of sex hormones affects bone development in growing puppies, particularly in large breeds. Studies have shown a reduction of bone mass in the spine and a delay in the closing of growth plates which, in turn, causes a lengthening of bones that are still growing and may

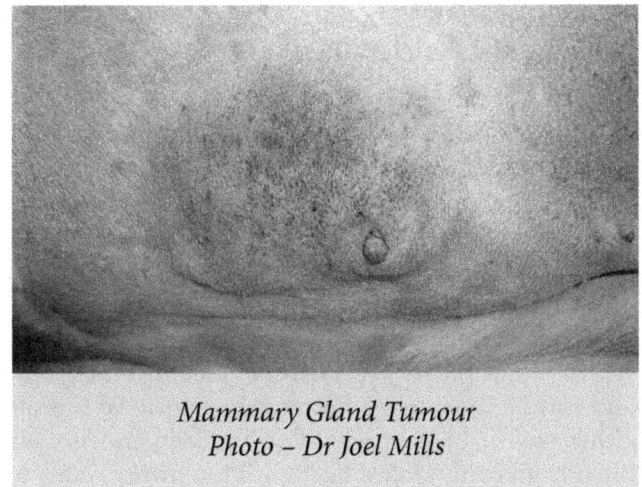

*Mammary Gland Tumour*
*Photo – Dr Joel Mills*

increase the risk of your dog developing hip dysplasia and other orthopaedic conditions. There also appears to be an increased risk of bone cancer in large breeds, particularly males. These potential problems don't pertain as strongly to the smaller breeds, however there may be other health issues such as an increased risk of hypothyroidism that you may like to consider. Sterilised dogs also need to have their weight monitored more carefully as they are more likely to become obese and therefore be at risk of the many health issues associated with obesity.

It is generally recommended that dogs are sterilised at six months of age. However, the likelihood of your dog being affected by any of the health risks associated with sterilisation may be reduced if males, in particular, are allowed to reach maturity before being neutered. You should consider though, that many male dogs that are left un-sterilised past maturity may be more likely to roam in search of females in heat, urinate on household items to mark territory, and not respond as well to training, particularly in group situations. It is advisable to discuss the pros and cons of sterilisation with your vet and breeder.

Females will come into oestrus, commonly referred to as 'heat' or 'season' every six to ten months. This lasts about three weeks and they will bleed quite heavily from the vagina for a reasonable portion of this time. For house dogs, this is messy and if the dog is kept outside there is always the risk of male dogs, attracted to the strong scent of a female on heat, breaking into your yard in an effort to become unwelcome fathers.

People often consider their dog's needs from a human perspective. They feel the need to have a family so they feel that it is cruel to deny their dog a family. In reality, dogs don't think the way we do. Raising a family lasts about four months from conception to weaning. After mating, the domesticated male dog has nothing to do with the process. The female endures nine weeks of pregnancy followed by six to eight weeks of nursing pups. In reality the novelty has generally worn off by four weeks when the pups have sharp teeth and claws

Done properly, breeding is an expensive exercise. Costs incurred by responsible registered breeders are high and include veterinary expenses that can entirely eliminate any profits made by the sale of the pups. Birth complications are commonplace and veterinary procedures such as Caesarean births are costly. The costs involved far outweigh the cost of sterilising your dog. To motivate people to get their dogs sterilised, many vets offer discounted procedures. If the health benefits and other reasons for sterilising your dog are not enough motivation for you, consider a visit to any dog rescue organisation, anywhere in the world. Literally millions of dogs are killed each year because homes cannot be found for them.

The procedure involves a general anaesthesia for both males and females. The procedure is best avoided in females that are in heat as the increased vascularity of the tissues does make the procedure a little riskier. The discomfort associated with the procedure is not long lasting, though your dog may need to wear a special collar, called an Elizabethan collar, for a week or two to prevent it being able to lick or pull out its stitches. Temporary chemical castration through the use of an implant is available as an alternative to permanent neutering for males. The implants are effective for six or twelve months depending on the type of implant used. This may be of benefit for those who have purchased a pedigree male and may be considering becoming a registered breeder in the future. Hormone treatments, either oral or in the form of an implant, are also available for bitches. These prevent the bitch from coming into heat until the owner wants to breed. If you are interested in these methods of contraception for your dog, whether male or female, you should discuss your options with your vet.

## Exercise and Play

If you think that your puppy's need to play will cease once it has matured, then you need to think again! It is true that as dogs grow older they become more sensible and may be less active, but the desire for a good game stays with most dogs for many years, provided that they remain healthy. I would consider a lack of playfulness in many dogs to be an early indicator of poor health, a pain issue, or weight related lethargy.

*Play and exercise helps to put your dog's energy to good use, keeping your dog fit and healthy.*

Dogs probably rival the Koala, in the number of hours they can spend sleeping each day. Unlike the latter, dogs generally eat a high protein, high energy diet which means that once awake they have energy to burn. In their wild ancestors, this energy would have been utilised hunting prey for their next meal. In domestic situations, this energy can become a truly destructive force if not redirected. Play and exercise helps to put this energy to good use, keeping your dog fit and healthy, as well as providing some mental stimulation for the dog.

Games are best varied to avoid compulsive behaviour such as presenting a ball or stick continuously for you to throw. Repetitive stereotypic behaviour is an indicator of boredom and difficult to eliminate once it has begun. Walking your dog every day is a good place to start, providing new and stimulating environments as well as exercise. A walk in the park, by a river, or a trip into the countryside can be pleasurable for both you and your dog. Of course, playing with children is always a favourite pastime but should always be supervised, particularly if the children are very young.

*Playing with children is always a favourite pastime but should always be supervised.*

Formal obedience training is another possibility and can have the added benefit of improving and developing your dog's behaviour through positive reinforcement. Obedience training can also be taken to competition level for those who enjoy the challenge of attaining recognised levels of achievement. Dogs can compete for awards from a basic level such as achieving their 'Companion Dog' award known as a 'CD' up to the level of obedience champion.

There are many dog clubs and organisations that schedule activities that can provide fun and exercise for both you and your dog. Activities are not restricted to purebred dogs and can include agility training, herding, jumping, and field work such as tracking and retrieving. Flyball is a sport that has become very popular with many dog owners. It involves teams of dogs racing against each other to be first across the line after jumping hurdles, triggering a mechanism to release a ball, retrieving the ball, and then returning with it over the hurdles. Most of these sports and activities have a competitive side to them so, like obedience training, many different award levels can be reached. The important thing to remember is that it is meant to be enjoyable - both for you and the dog! Your dog needn't become a champion to have fun participating in these activities. Size and breed is not a barrier either as even small dogs can compete in agility training.

*Agility training that includes jumps, tunnels and other obstacles is a popular sport for owners and dogs of all sizes.*

Most dogs just want to be with you so even if you don't have the time to participate in formal activities you need to allow them to become involved with your life. A dog will often follow their owner from room to room as they go about their daily business. A quick break for a short game is little to ask for such devotion.

*Most dogs just want to be with their owners A quick break for a short game is little to ask for such devotion.*

*The most obvious responsibility you have as a dog owner is to maintain the health, safety and well-being of your dog.*

# Common Health Issues

Rough Collie

## Introduction

The following health issues can affect any dog, regardless of breed or size. Some are age related acquired disorders but may also be the result of injury, obesity, poor diet and environmental factors. The likelihood of your dog developing one of these problems can be greatly reduced through providing a good diet and ensuring that your dog gets enough exercise to remain fit and active. Early diagnosis can be crucial in treating these conditions so a brief outline is provided to help you recognise a potential problem as early as possible.

## Arthritis

### What is arthritis?

Arthritis is inflammation of the joints. Large dogs are more likely to develop arthritis as they age. It can be caused by degenerative joint disease, injury such as tearing of the cruciate ligament, or poor bone development in growing dogs.

Degenerative joint disease can be both genetic, resulting from inherited conditions such as hip or elbow dysplasia, or it can develop from general health issues such as obesity, lack of exercise and poor diet. The condition develops as a result of damage to the slippery cartilage caps that cover the ends of bones within

Bouvier des Flandres Large dogs are more likely to develop arthritis as they age.

the joints, and which allow these bones to glide past each other with minimal friction. Often, it is damage to the synovial membrane, the sac surrounding the joints that causes the damage to the cartilage. This sac holds synovial fluid, which bathes and lubricates the joint. Without this, the joint does not move smoothly, the cartilage becomes roughened, and friction causes further damage leading to inflammation, pain and restricted movement.

## What are the signs or symptoms?

The symptoms are often very gradual in onset. Dogs may develop a limp in one or more limbs and be reluctant to engage in normal play and exercise. They may be slow to get up and be reluctant to climb stairs. Joints may be swollen or the dog may give a pain response to manipulation of the joints. Stiffness is often worse in the morning, improving during the day.

## How is it prevented?

Maintenance of joint health and prevention of joint degeneration will go a long way in preventing this condition. For purebred dogs there are now screening tests for breeding animals that allow responsible breeders to reduce the likelihood of arthritis associated with genetic conditions such as hip and elbow dysplasia from developing.

Regular exercise once a puppy's bone development is complete, feeding a good diet, maintaining ideal weight and preventing obesity will also help to prevent this condition from developing. There are also dietary additives that can be beneficial for older dogs by slowing the age related degenerative changes to the joints.

*Regular exercise, a good diet, maintaining ideal weight and preventing obesity will also help to prevent arthritis.*

## How is it diagnosed?

If you suspect your dog is showing symptoms you will need to visit your vet for a physical examination. X-rays will confirm arthritic changes to the joints. Joint fluid can also be analysed.

## How is it treated?

If the condition is the result of an injury such as tearing of the cruciate ligament, surgery will be required to stabilise the joint. The condition is then generally maintained with anti-inflammatory medications under the supervision of your vet. Anti-inflammatory medications are useful in relieving the pain associated with arthritis, but they don't repair the joint and can have serious side effects if used long term. Dietary supplements such as glucosamine with chondroitin, are useful for reducing inflammation and relieving pain. They also help rebuild the joint cartilage and synovial fluid and are much safer for long term use. It is important to use supplements that have been formulated to be absorbed by dogs. Acupuncture has also proved to be beneficial in the treatment of arthritic conditions.

# Cancer

## What is cancer?

Cancer is also known as neoplasia, a tumour or a growth. The study of cancer is called oncology. As the quality of veterinary care and general pet care increases, the life span of our dogs has also increased. This unfortunately means we are also seeing an increase in the prevalence of cancer in dogs. The American Veterinary Medical Association estimates that about 50% of all dogs over 10 years of age will be affected by cancer.

Cancer is an emotional subject – most of us have lost family or friends to cancer and it is just as devastating when we find our beloved dog has cancer. Good veterinary practitioners recognise this and will provide not only top quality care for your pet but will also provide emotional support for you as well. There are even veterinary oncologists now who specialise in this area. As with human cancer we are learning more about the various types of cancer and treatment options every day. However there are still a lot of unknowns, and in many cases, the prognosis for survival can be poor.

Cancer is effectively an uncontrolled growth of cells that can be inside or outside the body. The growth can cause destruction of local tissue, pain, inflammation, infection and damage to some of the body's organs. Paraneoplastic syndrome is another complication of cancer – this refers to conditions that occur distant to the tumour but as a direct result of the substances produced by the cancer. Examples are: hypoglycaemia (low blood glucose), anaemia, leukopenia (low white blood cell count) and even gastric ulcers. Thus cancer is a collection of hundreds of diseases that can affect all parts of the body, all species and all breeds of dog.

*Carcinoma (mast cell tumour) on the inner thigh. Photo - Dr Joel Mills*

Tumours can be benign or malignant. Benign cancer is an unchecked growth of cells that don't destroy body tissues (will not cause death or serious complications). However some benign tumours can make life difficult for dogs and require surgery. Lipomas are an example – these are fatty tumours that can make it difficult for the dog to move or function normally if the tumour is growing in an awkward area, for example, in the armpit. A malignant tumour causes local tissue destruction, organ damage and also has the potential for metastasis. Metastasis is when cancer cells spread from the initial tumour to a distant location in the body – common areas for metastasis are the lungs and the liver. The prognosis for a dog with a malignant tumour is more uncertain – however complete recovery can be made from some malignant cancers.

## What are the different types of cancer?

There are over 100 types of cancer. Some of the more common types are carcinoma, sarcoma and osteosarcoma. A carcinoma arises from the skin, mucous membranes and some organs such as the liver and kidneys. A sarcoma arises from the blood or bone cartilage. An osteosarcoma is a sarcoma originating in the bone.

Some examples of malignant tumours are:

- osteosarcoma (bone cancer)
- lymphoma (cancer of the lymph nodes)
- squamous cell carcinoma (commonly found in the mouth)
- adenocarcinoma (glandular tissue)
- mast cell tumour (appears on the skin)

Some examples of benign tumours are:

- lipoma (fatty cell tumour, common in the skin of older, overweight dogs)
- papilloma (wart-like tumour on the skin)
- adenoma (glandular tissue, anal adenomas are common in older dogs)

Mammary tumours are the most common neoplasia in female dogs – especially older entire bitches. Spaying or sterilising your bitch while still fairly young will greatly reduce the risk of mammary cancer. Benign mammary tumours can be successfully removed by surgery. Malignant mammary tumours may metastasise to the lungs and prognosis for these cases varies considerably.

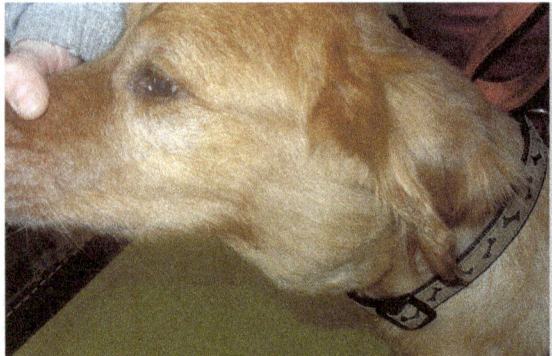

*Left - Lymphoma in a Golden Retriever.
Photo – Dr Joel Mills*

*Below - Carcinomas on the side.
Photo – Dr Joel Mills*

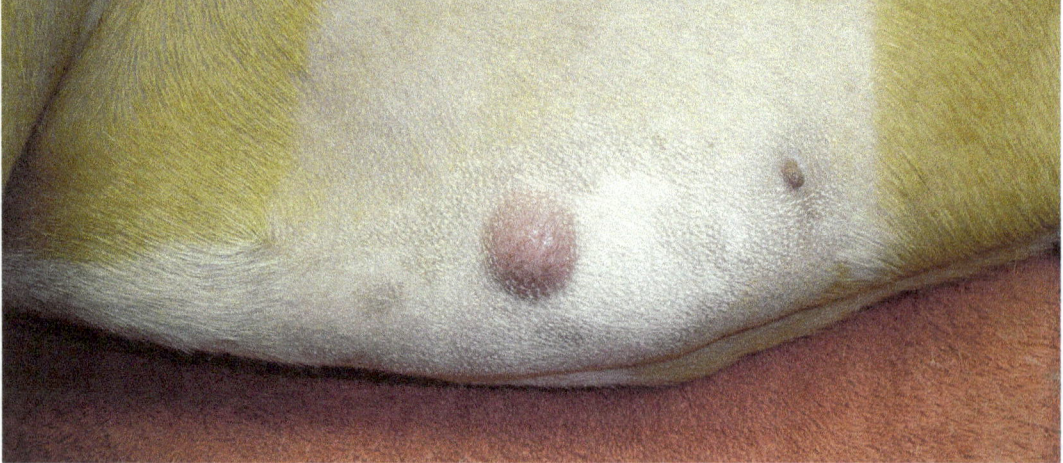

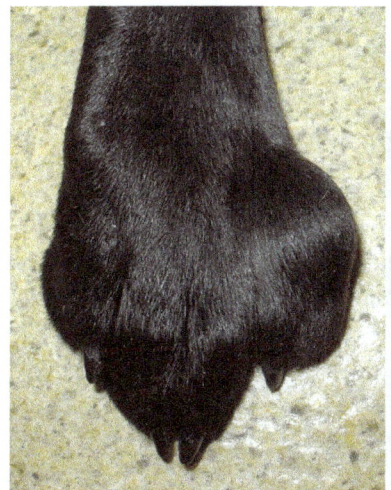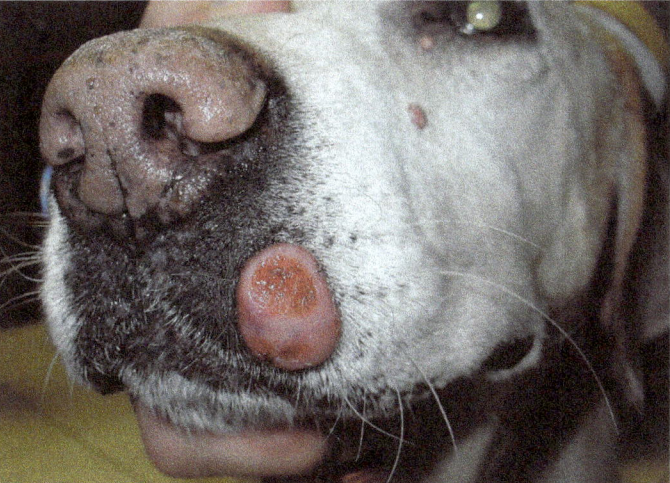

*Carcinomas on the toe and lips. Photo - Dr Joel Mills*

### What causes cancer?

As in human medicine, the causes are not fully understood. However some of the causes can be genetic, congenital, hormonal, viral, nutritional and traumatic. There may also be chemical and irradiation causes. Some breeds are more predisposed to some types of cancer than others but the genetic causes are not fully understood and there are no predictive tests available.

### What are the signs or symptoms?

Most dogs that develop cancer do so at about 6 – 15 years of age. Any unexplained lumps or bumps should be considered to be potential tumours and you should take your dog to the vet for examination. Osteosarcoma may present as pain and lameness in a limb. Some of the more serious tumours affecting internal organs may not show symptoms until the dog is feeling quite unwell. If in doubt, see your vet. Early diagnosis and intervention will greatly increase your dog's chances of survival and improve their quality of life.

### Ten Common Signs of Cancer in Small Animals

From the American Veterinary Medical Association - http://www.avma.org/

1. Abnormal swellings that persist or continue to grow
2. Sores that do not heal
3. Weight loss
4. Loss of appetite
5. Bleeding or discharge from any body opening
6. Offensive odour
7. Difficulty eating or swallowing
8. Hesitation to exercise or loss of stamina
9. Persistent lameness or stiffness
10. Difficulty breathing, urinating, or defecating

## How is cancer diagnosed?

Your dog will need a full veterinary examination including a complete blood screen, x-rays and ultrasound. Based on these results your vet may also recommend a fine needle aspirate (this is a collection of tumour cells obtained by inserting a small needle into the tumour), a biopsy (surgically taking a piece of the tumour to have it examined at the lab) or a bone marrow aspirate (collection of bone marrow). Depending on the type of tumour suspected and the resources of yourself and your veterinarian, they may even recommend a CT scan (computerised tomography) and MRI (magnetic resonance imaging). Diagnosis of cancer is not easy or cheap. Based on these results your vet will then have a reasonable idea of how bad the cancer is and be able to discuss with you potential treatment options and prognosis.

## What treatment is available?

Treatment options can be expensive and have severe side effects. It is vitally important that you have a good relationship with your veterinarian who can explain all of the benefits, complications and costs of each treatment. It is an emotional subject so it may be useful to bring a friend along with you to the consultation who may not be so emotionally involved and can help with keeping track of the discussion and asking questions. Give yourself time to think and do some additional research at home. The resources section of this book contains some internet sites that can provide helpful information.

- **Surgery** – can be an option to fully remove some types of tumours. Surgical options may also include amputation (for example of a limb affected with osteosarcoma) and cryosurgery (freezing of superficial tumours). Surgery may be a complete cure or simply palliative (extend the life of your dog and increase the quality of life remaining).
- **Chemotherapy** – this is treatment with chemical agents – often these agents are cytotoxic (destroy healthy tissue as well as cancerous) and administration usually requires hospitalisation and special care. Chemotherapy is often used after surgery.
- **Radiation Therapy** – this requires radiation of the tumour which can also affect healthy cells (similar to chemo). It can be used alone, or in conjunction with surgery and chemotherapy.
- **Hyperthermia** – local application of heat to tumours, often used in conjunction with radiotherapy.

Adjunctive therapy will also be required for cancer treatment – this may involve analgesia (pain relief), antibiotics, wound management and lots of tender loving care.

Cancer treatment is not always a realistic option for every dog and owner. It will require frequent, scheduled trips to the veterinary hospital and treatment at home. Often the treatment will persist for the rest of the dog's life. Treatment can sometimes result in remission – this means the clinical signs of the cancer no longer exist but the cancer itself is still present. This may occur for a short period (a few months) or over a year. At all times, the goal of cancer treatment is to improve your pet's quality of life, keeping it happy and pain free. At all times you will need to evaluate your dog's quality of life and be prepared to consider euthanasia when the time comes.

## Euthanasia

Depending on the severity of your dog's cancer, the treatment options and how your dog is likely to cope, even your financial resources – euthanasia is something you will need to consider. It is a difficult decision but such an important one. Sometimes the best thing we can do for our canine friends is to give them a calm and painless end. It is very important you do not feel pressured into this decision – it must be something you feel comfortable with. Ensure you have support available – people who do not have companion animals do not often recognise that when we lose them we experience the same degree of grief that we do for loved humans. There are some links to resources to help you with grief at the end of this book.

## How can I avoid buying a dog with a high potential for cancer?

As mentioned earlier, there are no genetic tests available to predict whether a dog will develop cancer. The best you can do is some research on the breed and discuss the family history with the breeder to determine if it has a higher risk of developing certain types of cancer. Unfortunately cancer is becoming more prevalent in dogs regardless of breed. Regular vet checks and monitoring of your pets health at home will help detect the problem earlier and therefore increase your dog's chances of survival.

# Cataracts

### What are cataracts?

Cataracts are opacities in the lens of the eye. The lens is a transparent disc which changes shape (via fine muscle control) to focus images onto the retina, where the signal is sent to the brain and interpreted as vision. Cataracts cause a loss in the transparency of the lens. Depending on the breed of the dog and the type of cataract, these opacities may be small and non-progressive, allowing your dog to see around them, causing minor loss of vision. However vision loss may be total if a cataract progresses to a larger size. Most cataracts have a genetic basis, and will be diagnosed when the dog is young.

- **Inherited cataracts**

    *Developmental / congenital* - these cataracts develop before the pup is born, and should be detectable via a veterinary examination once the pup's eyes are open, or by at least 8 weeks of age.

    *Juvenile / degenerative* - dogs with these cataracts are born with normal lenses, which then proceed to degenerate over time. They may develop anywhere between 8 weeks and 7 or 8 years of age, depending on the type of cataract (of which there are many), and also the breed of dog involved.

- **Non-inherited cataracts**

    *Senile* - these are associated with age, and may develop in any dog from the age of 8 or 9 years onwards. Disease - cataracts can be associated with the development of diseases such as diabetes mellitus.

    *Trauma or toxicity*

    *Nutritional deficiencies*

### What are the signs or symptoms?

You may notice your dog starting to bump into things or getting a milky, maybe bluish appearance to their eye.

### How is it diagnosed?

A simple eye examination by your veterinarian will detect cataracts, and often before any visual impairment has been noticed.

### How is it treated?

Occasionally, a congenital or early juvenile cataract may naturally reabsorb, and vision may improve. Some cataracts may also remain small and similarly require no intervention. However, in many cases the cataracts grow and cause severe vision impairment or blindness, and/or inflammation of the eye possibly leading to other severe eye disorders such as glaucoma or retinal detachment. The only treatment currently available to deal with a cataract is to surgically remove it, and possibly replace the lens with a plastic one. This requires the dog to undergo a general anaesthetic, but providing the eye is otherwise healthy, your dog is fit enough to cope with the anaesthetic and you can keep them quiet post-operatively, the improvement in vision can be excellent.

There are also some practical ways you can help your dog to cope with reduced vision. Dogs have terrific senses of smell and hearing, and this will help them to compensate for visual inadequacies, especially if you keep their environment stable. Don't move furniture around, keep paths clear of obstacles, and take regular routes when you take them on walks.

For some of the non-inherited cataracts, there are preventative measures you can take to reduce the risk of your dog even developing them. Maintaining good balanced nutrition is probably the best thing you can do. This will prevent deficiencies and also prevent obesity.

*You should keep a close eye on the clarity of your dog's eyes as they get older.*

### How can you avoid buying a dog with cataracts?

As congenital and juvenile cataracts are inherited, screening of the parents of a puppy you are considering purchasing is important. Make sure you obtain copies of certification showing a clear examination under one of the accredited eye schemes for the sire and dam of the puppy. A similar examination of your puppy at 8 weeks of age should also detect any congenital cataracts. Unfortunately, due to the late onset of symptoms for some of the juvenile cataracts, the sire and dam of your puppy may appear to be clear of the disease until they are well into or past their best breeding years, so if they were affected, you may not know it soon enough. If you are able to look further back through the pedigree of the parents, then this may improve your chances of detecting any evidence of juvenile cataracts in their lines. Responsible purebred breeders will generally have certification done on their breeding stock on an annual basis.

In the USA, the Canine Eye Registration Foundation (CERF) can direct you towards members of the American College of Veterinary Ophthalmologists for eye exams. In the UK, the British Veterinary Association (BVA) conducts eye exams, and in Australia, contact the Australian Veterinary Association (AVA) for examinations conducted under the Australian Canine Eye Scheme (ACES).

## Diabetes Mellitus (Type I Diabetes)

### What is diabetes?

Type I, or insulin dependent diabetes, is the most common form of diabetes occurring in dogs, and occurs when the body's ability to utilise carbohydrates and sugars is impaired. The hormone insulin (produced by the pancreas) regulates the uptake of sugars into cells throughout the body. Diabetes may mean that insulin is not being produced by the body or it is being produced but it is not being recognised and used appropriately. In some cases, there is a genetic predisposition for the body's immune system to destroy insulin producing cells.

In other cases, genes can make the dog more susceptible to diabetes in association with other factors such as obesity, illness or exposure to some drugs in large doses (corticosteroids or reproductive hormones). Without insulin, sugar builds up in the blood causing an array of problems. There is no cure for diabetes, but it can be controlled with insulin injections, diet and exercise. Once the disease begins your pet will need careful monitoring and insulin injections, usually twice a day, for the rest of its life. In many situations it is not possible or practical for people to adequately care for a diabetic dog.

### What are the signs or symptoms?

Symptoms may go unnoticed at first, as the onset of the disease is usually gradual. The first thing owners usually notice is that their dog is drinking more and more, and urinates all the time. Affected dogs will also be hungrier because they cannot utilise the sugar in their blood, but then tend to lose weight because they are burning body fat for energy almost exclusively. Fat can then accumulate in the liver. When blood sugar is about twice its normal level it enters the urine, causing excessive thirst and urination.

Long term problems include the development of cataracts, liver disease, pancreatitis and an increase in the occurrence of bacterial infections especially of the urinary tract. Persistent infections of the bladder and skin are common. If diabetes is left untreated, dogs will eventually develop ketoacidosis, a serious illness that can develop quite quickly, over a few days. Waste products called ketones build up as a result of fat metabolism and causes depression, vomiting, breathing problems and dehydration which lead to eventual coma or death. Treating ketoacidosis can be very expensive and may not be successful.

In severe cases of diabetes, signs are evident by six months of age. Affected puppies tend to eat and drink more than normal, but grow quite slowly. They urinate a lot and their faeces are soft. In later onset, diabetes does not develop until middle age. Signs include an increase in food and water intake and frequent urination combined with weight loss.

### How is it diagnosed?

If you suspect your dog is showing symptoms you will need a vet to perform a physical examination and test for sugar and ketone levels in the blood and urine.

### How is it treated?

If caught early and there are no other complications, insulin treatment, diet and exercise will balance out blood glucose levels and help minimise daily fluctuations. Daily injections up to twice a day may be required. If your dog's diabetes is due solely to obesity and there are no other complications, it should improve significantly or even fully recover once its weight is under control.

Complications from insulin treatment can occur if the dose is not right. If given too much insulin, hypoglycaemia or low blood sugar can occur. If not enough, secondary problems such as cataracts and liver disease may develop. If you are committed to helping your dog by carefully following a treatment plan provided by your vet, then your dog can still lead a happy, healthy long life.

### How can you avoid buying a dog with diabetes?

The mode of inheritance has not been established for all breeds, however, in some breeds, diabetes mellitus is an autosomal recessive trait, meaning that for an individual to be affected both parents are carriers of the gene or are affected themselves. Affected dogs should not be allowed to breed and their parents or siblings are also potential carriers.

Most dogs that are susceptible to diabetes will develop the disease after the age of five. If you are buying a dog rather than a puppy, then a general vet check should be performed before purchase if you are concerned about diabetes. If the dog is obese or has had pancreatic problems in the past it will be at greater risk of developing diabetes. Reproductive females are also at higher risk.

## Heart Disease

### What is heart disease?

Heart disease in dogs can either be congenital (present at birth) or age related (acquired heart disease) or related to parasitic infections (heartworm). Some breeds are also susceptible to a number of genetic heart conditions but the most common heart problems seen in dogs are age related and occur in the latter half of the dog's life. The two most common conditions are Mitral Valve Insufficiency and Dilated Cardiomyopathy.

1. **Mitral Valve Insufficiency** – This condition is most commonly associated with small dogs and results from the heart valves failing to close properly. Blood flows backwards into the heart chamber causing turbulence and is often first identified as a heart murmur.
2. **Dilated Cardiomyopathy** – This condition is most commonly associated with larger breeds. In this condition the muscular walls of the heart become thinner and weaken.

Both conditions result in a slowing of the passage of blood through the lungs. This results in fluid leaking out of the capillaries into the airways, resulting in a hacking cough. This cough is one of the first signs of congestive heart failure, where the body is unable to compensate for the heart's inability to supply adequate oxygen to the body tissues.

## What are the signs and symptoms?

As mentioned earlier, a heart murmur can indicate that a dog may be developing a problem. Difficulty breathing, a persistent cough that gets worse after exercise or at night, exercise intolerance, and lethargy may become more prevalent as the heart condition worsens. Symptoms of more advanced congestive heart failure include fainting, difficulty breathing while resting, and weight loss.

## How is it diagnosed?

A simple veterinary examination, where the vet listens to the dog's heart with a stethoscope, will help to identify heart disease in the early stages by listening for heart murmurs and abnormal lung sounds. More advance testing may include blood and urine tests to assess liver and kidney function, and chest x-rays can be taken to see if the heart is enlarged and if fluid in the lungs can be identified. A cardiac ultrasound is also used to determine the thickness of the heart walls and to assess the rate of contraction. Electrocardiograms (ECG) can be used to accurately determine the heart rate and identify abnormal rhythms.

*Some breeds, like Cavalier King Charles Spaniels, are susceptible to genetic heart conditions.*

## How is it treated?

Unfortunately, heart disease cannot be cured but it can be managed well. Early diagnosis will help to prolong your dog's life and greatly improve their quality of life. Maintaining a healthy weight and a good exercise regime will help to prevent the condition from developing, and will also reduce stress on heart of an affected animal.

However, excessive exercise for a dog with a heart condition can be dangerous. It is best to seek the advice of your vet for an effective heart management routine.

## Genetic Disease – An Introduction

Genetic disease is a health condition that is inherited by the offspring from one or both parents. It is carried by a gene that is present in the DNA strands in the cells. They are not infectious diseases that can pass from one animal to another by contact. It is important to note that any dog can carry disease that is associated with their genetic make-up. These diseases or health issues are not a problem associated with purebred dogs only. Dogs of different breeds may carry the same genetic fault and these faults will therefore pass to crossbred dogs as well. Due to the inbreeding that has occurred in the past, in order to establish the characteristics of that breed, some genetic diseases have become associated with particular breeds. However, the development of DNA testing and the controlled and documented breeding of purebred dogs have given responsible breeders the ability to recognise dogs that may carry defective genes. Good breeders are actively working to gradually eliminate these health issues from their breeding lines. Unfortunately, DNA testing is generally not practised by non-professional breeders of unregistered purebreds and crossbreds.

## Modes of Inheritance

It is important to understand how inherited diseases can be passed on, so you can make an informed decision regarding the purchase of a puppy. For example if you are not intending to breed with your dog, then it will be okay for it to be a carrier for a disease that is passed on via a recessive gene. Let me explain.

## Inheritance via an Autosomal Recessive Gene

This means that two copies of the abnormal gene must be present in an offspring in order for them to exhibit the disease. They must receive an abnormal gene from both the father and the mother. A dog with only one copy of the abnormal gene will not be affected by the disease, as its effects will have been 'masked' by the dominant normal gene. They will however be a carrier, and have the potential to pass the disease on to their offspring if bred with another carrier, or affected dog.

*Purebred dogs bred by reputable breeders that genetically test their dogs are sound and healthy.*

The patterns of how normal and abnormal genes are combined in a dog are described as their genotypes.

**Genotype A** - Genetically normal. Carries 2 normal genes - does not carry the gene for the disease.

**Genotype B** - Genetic carrier. Carries one normal gene and one abnormal gene either of which can be passed onto offspring. Carriers will not become affected themselves.

**Genotype C** - Genetically affected. Carries 2 disease genes, and will eventually exhibit symptoms of the disease. Will pass one gene for the disease on to all offspring, therefore all offspring will be either affected or carriers.

The following table shows the probable outcome of breeding with dogs of different genotypes.

| Dam ↓ / Sire → | Genotype A Normal Unaffected | Genotype B Carrier Unaffected | Genotype C Affected |
|---|---|---|---|
| Genotype A Normal Unaffected | Genotype A Normal Unaffected | 50% Type A / 50% Type B | Genotype B Carrier Unaffected |
| Genotype B Carrier Unaffected | 50% Type A / 50% Type B | 25% Type A / 50% Type B / 25% Type C | 50% Type B / 50% Type C |
| Genotype C Affected | Genotype B Carrier Unaffected | 50% Type B / 50% Type C | Genotype C Affected |

You may find that breeders will breed from carriers, and sometimes even from affected animals if they have other traits that are particularly valuable. It is crucial that these carriers and affected dogs are only bred to unaffected Genotype A dogs to prevent producing affected offspring. Over time, they can keep breeding carriers back to normal unaffected dogs thereby eventually eliminating the disease gene while retaining the desirable characteristics found in a particular genetic line. In the process of doing this, a number of carriers will be produced. These will be perfectly healthy, but a breeder may insist that they only go to homes where they won't be bred. If a puppy you are considering purchasing is the product of one of these crosses, then the above information will help you to understand the process and allow you to make a more informed decision.

### Inheritance via a Sex-linked Recessive Gene

Some recessively inherited traits are sex-linked. This means that the genes in question are found on the X-chromosome. Females have two X-chromosomes and males have an X and a Y. The Y-chromosome is incapable of carrying a normal gene to mask the effect of the recessive gene. Therefore, females require two copies of the abnormal gene to be affected, whereas males require only one.

### Inheritance via a Dominant Gene

This means that only one copy of the abnormal gene needs to be present in an offspring for them to exhibit the disease. It's a lot easier to eliminate these diseases, as they can't be hidden in carriers, although there are still challenges as some aren't expressed until later in life, when dogs may be well into or past their best breeding years.

*The likelihood of your dog developing one of these problems can be greatly reduced through good diet and exercise.*

# Responsible Ownership

The most obvious responsibility you have as a dog owner is to maintain the health and well-being of your dog. Providing health care, both physical and emotional, fresh food, water, and shelter are the minimum requirements of owning a dog. In addition, you must also take responsibility for shaping your dog's behaviour and ensuring that it does not impact negatively on members of your family, human and animal, as well as other people and the environment. Dogs will learn throughout their lives regardless of whether or not we teach them. Left to their own devices they are more likely to learn to do things that impact negatively on their owners. With a little effort their ability to learn can be used to shape good behaviour instead.

*Lakeland Terrier*

## Basic Training and Obedience

Shaping your dog's behaviour is much easier with a basic understanding of positive reinforcement training. Positive reinforcement involves rewarding your dog for good behaviour both with food or toys and by giving plenty of praise and attention. Bad behaviour is either ignored, or corrected by immediate intervention, redirecting and teaching the dog what to do instead. Control of your animal is your primary goal but developing a level of understanding between you and your dog can have great rewards, and prevent a considerable amount of stress resulting from coping with bad behaviour in your dog.

*Developing a level of understanding between you and your dog can have great rewards.*

The principles of positive reinforcement training are relatively simple to learn but you need to be careful where you go for advice. Many people have different methods of training and often punishment is recommended. It may seem like the logical thing to do as we are angry at our dogs for what they have done and, at the time, it seems to be the appropriate response. Unfortunately, punishment can often exacerbate the situation rather than improve it and also lead to your dog responding to you with fear and mistrust.

An example of inappropriate punishment is the suggestion that if your dog urinates inside you should rub its nose in it. Rubbing its nose in something it did earlier will make no sense to the dog. The dog will only understand that all of a sudden, without provocation, its owner got really nasty and attacked it. The dog is more likely to associate the punishment with what it was doing at the time you became angry. You can see the reason for confusion if the dog was lying quietly at the time you unleashed your anger. You will be far more successful in the long run by positively reinforcing your dog for urinating outside. When dogs realise that they are rewarded by their owner for certain behaviours, they are far more likely to perform those behaviours in the future. You must remember to give your dog lots of attention, even if it isn't being asked to perform a task. Dogs that are ignored frequently begin to misbehave simply to get attention. In their minds, negative attention, such as a verbal reprimand, is still attention, so if misbehaving gets you to notice them, in their minds it might be worth it. Although there may be other causes, timid, fearful and aggressive dogs are typical of those that have been the recipients of repeated punishment.

*Socialisation helps to create well adjusted dogs that can interact with others.*

Socialisation through exposure to a variety of dogs, other animals, people, and situations helps to create well adjusted dogs. To be able to socialise your dog properly it needs to be controlled. Obedience and behavioural training can be taken to high levels of achievement but some of the basic commands that your dog needs to learn in order to remain in control in public are as follows.

**Watch** is a simple but effective command to get your dog's attention. It is crucial for successful training to be able to get your dog to focus on you. It makes giving other commands easier as the dog is already waiting for a response from you. Stating the word 'watch', combined with pointing to your face and rewarding the dog when it makes eye contact is all that is required to learn this command.

**Recall** is one of the most important basic commands that should be learned, particularly if you wish to allow your dog off lead in public. If your dog tends to run away, keep it on a long line so that you can practice many controlled recalls, and reward your dog every time it comes back to you. As frustrating as it is that your dog has run away, punishing it on its return will only teach the dog NOT to come back at all. Eventually with consistent training and reward, the dog will not only come back when called but will be less likely to leave in the first place.

**Sit** is probably one of the most effective commands for gaining control over your dog. Once a dog's rear end is on the ground it is unable to move away from you or jump up. One aspect of obedience training involves teaching your dog to walk quietly at your side without pulling. With your dog controlled by your side while walking on a loose leash, it is then easy, for safety purposes, to teach your dog to sit when you come to a road, or to sit quietly by your side while you talk to friends that you might meet during your walk.

**Drop** is an extension of the 'sit' command and like 'sit' is a great way of controlling your dog. The drop position is very submissive and in drop position the dog is even more restricted in movement.

**Wait or Stay** is used to ask your dog to remain in one spot while you walk away. 'Stay' is used if the dog is being asked to remain in one position for long periods. It allows the dog to relax while it waits. 'Wait' is used when you want the dog to hold the position for a shorter time. This command allows you to maintain the dog's attention until the next command is given. A dog being asked to 'Wait' will expect another command to follow and should watch its owner intently while it waits.

*'Sit' is probably one of the most effective commands for gaining control over your dog.*

Responsible Ownership 159

Remember to always release your dog from the task you have given it. By failing to release your dog with a command such as - 'Okay…..Good dog!' your dog will be forced to make up its own mind about when the behaviour is no longer required. This leads to ambiguity and confusion. With positive reinforcement training the timing is very important. Commands must be clear and the dog rewarded immediately when the behaviour is performed. Verbal praise should always be given in addition to food rewards as this will eventually replace some of the need for food rewards. Other devices such as training clickers or whistles can be used. These are used to mark the correct behaviour at the precise moment the dog performs it. Food can then be immediately given to the dog as a reward. The dog will eventually associate the sound with having successfully completed a task. One of the benefits of using this technique is that, with further training, clickers and whistles can be used as a 'bridge'. 'Bridging' is useful when the dog is working at a distance and can't be given a food reward immediately. Food or a reward that the dog really loves must follow the bridge as closely as possible. Because the dog associates the sound with having successfully completed a task, the bridge is both an immediate indication of "well done", plus a promise of food rewards to come. Avoid repeating commands; otherwise your dog will learn that it is not important to comply with the first request. It is easy to make a mistake in training that can take a long time to correct. It helps to attend formal training classes with a reputable qualified instructor or behaviourist. You can also find links in the Resources section at the end of the book to more detailed training information.

*'Stay' is used if the dog is being asked to remain in one position for long periods.*

## Being a Good Neighbour

Acquiring a dog or puppy should not mean that your neighbours have also acquired a dog. It is your responsibility to make sure that your dog does not impact adversely on your neighbour's quality of life. You should familiarise yourself with local regulations with regard to dog ownership before acquiring a dog. Your dog should be secured within your property and your fences should prevent accidental entry, particularly by neighbouring children. They should also prevent the dog from escaping to roam the streets and defecate on neighbour's lawns or damage their gardens. If your dog is not confined it may intimidate people walking past or attack other dogs being walked by their owners.

Barking is one of the most common complaints from neighbours and it can become a serious dispute. Barking when the owner is away is often the major problem. Due to the fact that their dog is not noisy when they are home, many people will not acknowledge their neighbours' complaints. It is important to keep communication open with your neighbours to avoid animosity. Voice activated recorders are a simple way of determining how bad the

*Activity and puzzle toys may help to keep your dog busy and quiet while you are away from home.*

*Remember, some squeaky toys can be as annoying to neighbours as barking.*

barking problem is after you have left the property.

Barking may be attention seeking or result from the dog's natural desire to protect its territory. Well socialised dogs that are used to lots of people, noises, and other animals may be less likely to become alarm barkers, inclined to bark at the slightest disturbance. It may also result from boredom, frustration, and separation anxiety when their owner is away from home. Sometimes it can result from health issues, particularly in older dogs. Providing enrichment for your dog in the form of activity toys can be helpful in occupying them. But remember, some noisy 'squeaky' toys can be as annoying as barking! Puzzle toys and 'Kongs™' allow you to hide treats inside. Retrieving the treats can occupy a dog for long periods so they may be a better choice. It is important to make sure that toys are the appropriate size for your dog so they are not at risk from choking while you are away.

Getting them used to being outside on their own while you are home can avoid separation anxiety and help them relax while you are away. They should be provided with a comfortable, secure area to spend the day. The company of another dog may also help. Dogs can play together for long periods and the security of having another dog around can help those that bark as a result of separation anxiety. You must be aware, however, that two dogs can mean 'double trouble', particularly where the problem is alarm barking. It is natural pack behaviour for dogs to join in the defence of their territory.

*The company of another dog can help to keep some dogs relaxed and quiet while you're out but two dogs can also be 'double trouble'! Above - Salukis  Below - Irish Terriers*

It is important not to reward inappropriate barking. While it may be acceptable for dogs to bark to alert their owners to the arrival of strangers, it should be stopped quickly before the dog (or the neighbour) becomes too agitated. Other incidences of inappropriate barking should be ignored. Acknowledging your dog's barking, even by approaching it to try and stop the barking, can reward and reinforce the behaviour. However, if the barking is alarm barking, it is probably better to investigate what the dog is barking at before asking it to stop. Many barking problems can be corrected through training but some problems may be more difficult and may require the assistance of an animal behaviourist or professional trainer. To be able to correct the problem, it is important to be able to identify the cause or motivation for the barking, and recognise any reinforcement that may be being provided by the owner. Before becoming defensive, try and consider your neighbours situation and implement some changes or training to help alleviate the problems that are being experienced.

## Respecting Wildlife and the Environment

As a dog owner you are totally responsible for the actions and safety of your dog. Dogs should never be walked off lead along roads and in heavily populated areas. This is as much for their safety as it is for the safety of others. Dogs are easily distracted and even extremely well trained dogs may defy their owners if something like another dog or cat attracts them without warning. They may run out into traffic, injuring themselves, or others, by causing an accident. They may also make it difficult for other people walking their dogs to be able to control them, if they are being approached or harassed, even in play, by a dog off lead.

Once you are in less populated and safer areas such as parks, you can allow your dog off lead for a run or game of fetch, provided that you have enough control to ensure that your dog will return on demand, so that it does not get lost, or approach and interfere with other people who may be enjoying the park or a walk in the bush. Cleaning up after your dog is also important. Areas that are heavily contaminated with dog faeces are a breeding ground for disease and parasites. Parks and public open spaces are for the enjoyment of everyone and stepping in dog waste is unpleasant, unacceptable, and may be a threat to the health of visitors, especially children. Many places are banning dogs because people are not adhering to simple requests for dog owners to clean up after their dogs. In the long run, irresponsible behaviour disadvantages everyone. Unless you know that there will be 'poo bags' provided at the park you are visiting you should always carry some bags with you to help you remove and properly dispose of your dog's waste.

Beaches are another place where you must consider the rights of others using the beach. There are often beach areas set aside for use by people with dogs. It is important to use these areas and

*Being a responsible dog owner means cleaning up after your dog in public places.*

Responsible Ownership

*You need to be vigilant at the beach when your dog is in the surf or interacting with other dogs.*

again, clean up after your dog. Many dogs enjoy the surf and getting wet seems to wind them up making them more excitable, and perhaps uncontrollable! Beaches can also pose a safety risk to dogs, particularly breeds that love to swim. Sharks are particularly attracted to dogs and the strength of the surf itself is a concern. You need to be vigilant when your dog is at the beach and in the water.

A well fenced yard with solid panels will help protect wildlife from your dog. They are not foolproof however, as many native animals can climb or squeeze through small gaps. Domestic dogs and cats can impact heavily on the populations of some native animals. Off-lead and in the yard, you need to keep a watchful eye on your dog's behaviour whenever possible. In many instances this can be as much for the protection of your dog as it is for the protection of native animals. In areas where rabies is prevalent you must make sure that your dog is protected from contracting the disease from a wild animal bite. Ensuring that you keep vaccinations up to date is for your protection as well as that of the dog. Dogs infected with rabies may bite their owners and infect them, even if they were totally trustworthy before contracting the disease. By the time the disease is diagnosed it is likely to be fatal for both dog and owner. Depending on where you live, your dog may be at serious risk of snake bite and dogs that are suspected of being bitten need immediate attention if the administration of antivenene is to be effective. If you live in an area frequented by dangerous animals such as bears and large cats, you should make sure they are safe from becoming prey.

The veterinary costs of unfortunate encounters with wildlife can be extremely high. Antivenene is expensive and treating any injuries can cause pain and discomfort to your wallet, as well as to the dog. For all concerned, monitoring your dog's activities, when encounters with wildlife are possible, is the best course of action.

## Irresponsible Practices

It might seem like common sense to many of us, but dogs are killed and injured each year as a result of a number of irresponsible practices. Dogs should never be left in hot cars as dehydration and death can occur in a short period of time. Heat can also result in burns to the pads of dogs' feet while being exercised on the pavement on a hot day, or even at home while running around swimming pools. They are often excited enough by the activities of their owners in the pool, not to notice the heat in their tough pads until much later. Leaving dogs unrestrained on the back of open vehicles and trucks can easily result in the dog falling off, injuring itself or being run over by following traffic. Tethering your dog to the back of a vehicle and allowing enough lead for the dog to fall and hang itself, or be dragged, is equally stupid. A well trained, trustworthy dog may run well alongside a bicycle, but many are not trained well enough to guarantee that they will not become distracted suddenly by something like another animal. In their rush to greet or attack the other animal they may run into the wheel or drag their owner across the road into oncoming traffic. You should also be aware of their fatigue level as they may not be able to run for as long as you can ride. To keep your dog safe, you simply need to think about what you are doing with your dog and the potential consequences of your actions if things go wrong.

## Old Age

Unfortunately, dogs age much faster than we do so we are often forced to watch our companion suffer the effects of old age, long before we would like to. We have already covered some health issues associated with older dogs as well as discussing dietary and exercise options that may help to prolong your dog's life. The important thing to remember is that the effects of old age will need to be addressed at some stage and this should therefore be taken into consideration. Older dogs may need to be kept warmer, may need more veterinary care incurring additional costs, be more inclined to have toileting accidents and, in general, require a little more patience. If you are not prepared to meet the financial costs, as well as the potential inconvenience of dealing with an older dog, you should think carefully about your decision to become a dog owner.

*Old age is an inevitable part of owning a dog.*

*New toy .... happy old boy!*

# References & Resources

*Smooth Coat Chihuahua*

## General Resources

### National Kennel Clubs and Councils

**American Kennel Club (AKC)**
http://www.akc.org

**Australian National Kennel Council (ANKC)**
http://www.ankc.org.au

**Canadian Kennel Club (CKC)**
http://www.ckc.ca

**Continental Kennel Club (CKC)**
http://www.continentalkennelclub.com

**Kennel Club of Great Britain (KCGB)**
http://www.thekennelclub.org.uk

**National Kennel Club (NKC)**
http://www.nationalkennelclub.com

**New Zealand Kennel Club (NZKC)**
http://www.nzkc.org.nz

**United Kennel Club (UKC)**
http://www.ukcdogs.com

**World Canine Organisation
(Fédération Cynologique Internationale – FCI)**
http://www.fci.be

### Dog Clubs and Clubs for the Mixed Breeds

**Agility Dog Association of Australia (ADAA)**
http://www.adaa.com.au/index.htm

**American Canine Hybrid Club**
http://www.achclub.com/index.php

**Crossbreed and Mongrel Club (United Kingdom)**
http://www.crossbreed-and-mongrel-club.org.uk/

**Mixed Breed Dog Clubs of America**
http://mbdca.tripod.com/

**Dog Breed Clubs, Societies & Associations Directory**
http://www.animalinfo.com.au/listings/index/2/5

**Dog Sports Clubs, Societies and Associations Directory**
http://www.animalinfo.com.au/listings/index/2/24

## Training Resources

**Positive Reinforcement Training with Canine Connection LLC**
http://www.dubuquedogtraining.com/
http://www.animalinfo.com.au/listings/view/2/16/271/l:Positive+Reinforcement+Training+with+Canine+Connection+LLC

**Positive Reinforcement Training for Dogs**
http://www.animalinfo.com.au/fact_sheets/index/2/25

**Dog Behaviour Fact Sheets from Animalinfo**
http://www.animalinfo.com.au/fact_sheets/index/2/9

**Dog Training and Sports Fact Sheets from Animalinfo**
http://www.animalinfo.com.au/fact_sheets/index/2/8

**Dog Trainers & Dog Behaviorists Directory**
http://www.animalinfo.com.au/listings/index/2/16

## Additional General Resources

**Dog Information, Products and Resources**
http://www.animalinfo.com.au/animals/index/2

**Dog Breed Info Center**
http://www.dogbreedinfo.com

**Dog Infomat**
http://www.doginfomat.com

**Dog Owner's Guide**
http://www.canismajor.com/dog/index.html

Fogle, B. 2006. Dogs – Eyewitness Companions. Dorling Kindersley Ltd., London.

Mehus-Roe, K. (ed.) 2005. Dog Bible

The Definitive Source for All Things Dog. BowTie Press, California.

**Pedigree – We're for Dogs**
www.pedigree.com.au

**QualityDogs.com**
http://www.qualitydogs.com

Sylvester P. (ed.) 1989. The Readers Digest Illustrated Book of Dogs.

The Readers Digest Association, Inc., New York. Taylor, D. 1986. You and Your Dog. Dorling Kindersley Ltd., London.

**Wikipedia -Dog**
http://en.wikipedia.org/wiki/Dog
http://en.wikipedia.org/wiki/Origin_of_the_domestic_dog

**New Finding Puts Origins of Dogs in Middle East**
http://www.nytimes.com/2010/03/18/science/18dogs.html?_r=1

# Health Resources

## Disease Testing and Information Organisations

### UNITED STATES

### Health Registries

**Canine Eye Registration Foundation (CERF)**
http://www.vmdb.org/cerf.html

This register provides a list of pure-bred dogs that have been examined by members of the American College of Veterinary Ophthalmologists (ACVO), and been found to be free of heritable eye disease.

**Orthopedic Foundation for Animals (OFA)**
http://www.offa.org

This foundation provides numerous databases documenting the disease status of dogs. Originally concentrating on hip dysplasia, they have now expanded their range of databases to include others, such as elbow dysplasia, patella luxation, cardiac disease, shoulder OCD and an increasing number of breed specific congenital diseases based on DNA results.

**Canine Health Information Centre (CHIC)**
http://www.caninehealthinfo.org/

This organisation collects health histories and genetic material (blood or cheek cells) in order to assist in research towards improving canine health. They also provide a centralised database which consolidates health screening results from a number of different sources, including the OFA and CERF databases.

**CNM online!**
http://www.labradorcnm.com/

Maintains an international registry of Labradors that have tested clear for Centronuclear Myopathy.

**University of Pennsylvania Hip Improvement Program (PennHIP)**
http://www.pennhip.org

The Veterinary School at the University of Pennsylvania developed a technique for detecting Hip Dysplasia, called the PennHIP method. Certified PennHIP trained veterinarians from around the world send X-rays for assessment. Results are added to a database. Their main objective is to reduce the incidence and severity of Hip Dysplasia.

### Testing Agencies

**Optigen**
http://www.optigen.com

Provides DNA-based testing services

**VetGen**
http://www.vetgen.com

Provides DNA-based testing services

**PennGen Laboratories**
http://research.vet.upenn.edu/penngen/PennGenHome/tabid/91/Default.aspx

**HealthGene**
http://healthgene.com/canine/

The OFA website can also provide the location of laboratories certified to provide DNA-based testing.

## ENGLAND

## Health Registries

**The Kennel Club of Great Britain**
www.thekennelclub.org.uk

Results from the British Veterinary Association's (BVA) hip, elbow and eye examinations are recorded on the Kennel Club's database. The Kennel Club also works in conjunction with a number of laboratories to provide a database of results for an increasing number of conditions detectable via DNA screening.

## Testing Agencies

**British Veterinary Association (BVA)**
http://www.bva.co.uk

The BVA runs a number of health certification schemes in conjunction with the Kennel Club of Great Britain. They run an Elbow Dysplasia Scheme, a Hip Dysplasia Scheme, and in conjunction with the International Sheep Dog Society (ISDS), an Eye Scheme. The Kennel Club of Great Britain can provide the location of laboratories certified to provide DNA-based testing.

**Animal Health Trust**
http://www.aht.org.uk

Also enquire at Optigen for agencies in Europe that will provide transport of samples to the USA for testing  www.optigen.com

## AUSTRALIA

## Health Registries

**Australian National Kennel Council (ANKC)**
http://www.ankc.org.au

Results from the Australian Veterinary Association's (AVA) hip, elbow and eye schemes (ACES and CHEDS) are recorded on the Kennel Council's database.

## Testing Agencies

**Australian Veterinary Association (AVA)**
http://www.ava.com.au

The AVA runs a number of health certification schemes in conjunction with the Australian National Kennel Council. They run an eye scheme (Australian Canine Eye Scheme –

ACES), as well as a Hip and Elbow Dysplasia Scheme (Canine Hip and Elbow Dysplasia Scheme – CHEDS).

**Genetic Technologies Ltd.**
http://www.gtg.com.au/

This company runs the Australian Canine Pedigree Assurance Programme (ACPAP), which provides DNA profiling services such as determining parentage and screening for genetic diseases. The programme is endorsed by the Australian National Kennel Council (ANKC).

**Gen Test (Vetgen representative)**
http://members.optusnet.com.au/gentest/

## National Veterinary Associations

**Australian Veterinary Association (AVA)**
http://www.ava.com.au

**British Veterinary Association (BVA)**
http://www.bva.co.uk

**American Veterinary Medical Association (AVMA)**
http://www.avma.org/

## Further Reading

**Canine Inherited Disorders Database**
http://www.upei.ca/~cidd/intro.htm

Canine Inherited Disorders Database. A very comprehensive site giving details of genetic disorders and breed predispositions

**The Dog Food Project**
http://www.dogfoodproject.com/

**The Merck Veterinary Manual Seventh Edition Ed. Clarence M Fraser Merck & Co., Inc. 1991 USA Also available free online at**
http://www.merckmanuals.com/vet/index.html

**Dog Health Fact Sheets from Animalinfo**
http://www.animalinfo.com.au/fact_sheets/index/2/3

## Pet Loss Support

**Cornell University Pet Loss Support Hotline**
http://www.vet.cornell.edu/Org/PetLoss/
http://www.cvm.uiuc.edu/CARE/

**Association for Pet Loss and Bereavement**
http://www.aplb.org/

**AVMA Pet Loss Help**
http://www.avma.org/KB/Resources/Reference/human-animal-bond/Pages/Human-Animal-Bond-grief-euthanasia.aspx

## Cancer Information

**Animal Cancer Center**
http://www.csuanimalcancercenter.org/

**Animal Cancer Foundation**
http://www.animalcancer.org/

**The Canine Cancer Project (includes canine cancer support groups)**
http://www.caninecancerproject.com/

**Land of Pure Gold Foundation**
http://cancer.landofpuregold.com/

Very comprehensive site with support resources also

**Wing-N-Wave Labradors**
http://www.labbies.com/cancerintro.htm

Very comprehensive resource site for info on canine cancer

**About.com: Veterinary Medicine**
http://vetmedicine.about.com/cs/dogdiseasesc/a/dogcancer.htm

## Additional Health Resources

**American Heartworm Society**
http://www.heartwormsociety.org/CanineHeartwormInfo.htm

**Black's Veterinary Dictionary 17th Edition**
Ed Geoffrey West  A&C Black. London 1992  London.

**Canada's Guide to Dogs**
http://www.canadasguidetodogs.com/health/tvd.htm

**Canine Arthritis by Anthony Coyne MVB MRCVS Animal Herb Company**
http://vetmedicine.about.com/library/viewers/uc-arthritis.htm

**Canine Epilepsy Resources**
http://www.canine-epilepsy.com/

**CavalierHealth.org**
http://www.cavalierhealth.org/index.html

**Clinical Textbook for Veterinary Technicians  Third Edition**
Dennis M. McCurnin WB Saunders Co. 1994  Philadelphia, London, Toronto, Montreal, Sydney, Tokyo.

**Collins Dictionary of Biology  Second Edition**
WG Hale, JP Margham and VA Saunders  Harper Collins Publishers 1995  Great Britain.

**Cornell College of Veterinary Medicine**
http://www.vet.cornell.edu/consultant/consult.asp

**Doctors Foster and Smith**
http://www.drsfostersmith.com/

**Dog Owner's Guide**
http://www.canismajor.com/dog/vaccine.html#Intro

**Dogsites**
http://www.dogsites.com.au/

**Fitsimmons, L. An Explanation of the International Elbow Working Group Grading Scheme. In: Online-Vets**

**Goodwin, J.K. 1997. Atrioventricular Valve Dysplasia. In:**

Tilley, L.P. & Smith, F.W.K. The 5 Minute Veterinary Consult. pp 380-381. Williams & Wilkins, Baltimore.

**The Illustrated Veterinary Guide for Dogs, Cats, Birds and Exotic Pets**

Chris C. Pinney, DVM, TAB Books (McGraw-Hill Inc), 1992 USA

**Institute for Genetic Disease Control**
http://www.gdcinstitute.org/

**Lavelle, R. Elbow Disease in Growing Dogs.**
http://www.siriusdog.com/elbow-uap-fcp-dysplasia.htm

**Long-term Health Risks and Benefits Associated with Spay/Neuter in Dogs.**

Laura J Sanborn, MS. May 14, 2007.
http://www.naiaonline.org/pdfs/LongTermHealthEffectsOfSpayNeuterInDogs.pdf

**Mar Vista Animal Medical Center**
http://www.marvistavet.com/index.html

**Nasisse, M.P & Miller, P.E. (ed.) 1997. Cataracts.**

In: Tilley, L.P. & Smith, F.W.K. The 5 Minute Veterinary Consult. pp 428-429. Williams & Wilkins, Baltimore.

**Pickett, J.P. & Miller, P.E. (ed.) 1997. Ectropion.**

In: Tilley, L.P. & Smith, F.W.K. The 5 Minute Veterinary Consult. p 537. Williams & Wilkins, Baltimore.

**Pickett, J.P. & Miller, P.E. (ed.) 1997. Entropion.**

In: Tilley, L.P. & Smith, F.W.K. The 5 Minute Veterinary Consult. p 556. Williams & Wilkins, Baltimore.

**Plant, J.D. & Ackerman, L. (ed.) 1997. Atopy.**

In: Tilley, L.P. & Smith, F.W.K. The 5 Minute Veterinary Consult. pp 376-377. Williams & Wilkins, Baltimore.

**Schwartz, P.D. 1997. Osteochondrodysplasia.**

In: Tilley, L.P. & Smith, F.W.K. The 5 Minute Veterinary Consult. pp 886-887. Williams & Wilkins, Baltimore.

**Textbook of Veterinary Internal Medicine 6th Edition**

Ed. Stephen J. Ettinger W.B. Saunders Company 2005 Philadelphia, London, Toronto.
University of California - William R. Pritchard Veterinary Medical Teaching Hospital

http://www.vmth.ucdavis.edu/vmth/clientinfo/info/genmed/vaccinproto.html

**Veterinary Pet Care.com**
http://www.veterinarypetcare.com/heart.html

**Veterinary technician Vol 20, No. 2 February 1999 Hip Dysplasia – Notes for Owners and breeders**

**Veterinary Nursing (Formerly Jones's Animal Nursing, 5th Edition)**
Edited by DR Lane and B Cooper  Book 1 and 2,  Elsevier Science Ltd.,  1994  Uk, USA, Japan.

**Vetinfo – A Veterinary Information Service**
http://www.vetinfo.com/

**West Boulevard Veterinary Clinic**
http://www.wbvc.bc.ca

**Wikipedia - Infectious_canine_hepatitis**
http://en.wikipedia.org/wiki/Infectious_canine_hepatitis

**Working Dogs Cyberzine**
http://www.workingdogs.com/vcpatlux.htm

## Other Titles from Animalinfo Publications

**Getting to Know Labradors - A Guide to Choosing and Owning a Labrador**
http://www.animalinfo.com.au/products/view/2/6/9

**Getting to Know Beagles - A Guide to Choosing and Owning a Beagle**
http://www.animalinfo.com.au/products/view/2/6/15

**Getting to Know Dobermanns - A Guide to Choosing and Owning a Dobermann**
http://www.animalinfo.com.au/products/view/2/6/23

**Getting to Know Cavaliers - A Guide to Choosing and Owning a Cavalier King Charles Spaniel**
http://www.animalinfo.com.au/products/view/2/6/21

**Getting to Know Staffords - A Guide to Choosing and Owning a Staffordshire Bull Terrier**
http://www.animalinfo.com.au/products/view/2/6/16

**Getting to Know Poodles - A Guide to Choosing and Owning a Poodle**
http://www.animalinfo.com.au/products/view/2/6/20

**Getting to Know German Shepherds - A Guide to Choosing and Owning a German Shepherd Dog**
http://www.animalinfo.com.au/products/view/2/6/26

**Getting to Know English Cockers: A Guide to Choosing and Owning an English Cocker Spaniel**
http://www.animalinfo.com.au/products/view/2/6/22

www.ingramcontent.com/pod-product-compliance
Lightning Source LLC
Chambersburg PA
CBHW081110080526
44587CB00021B/3536